RUDOLF STEINER (1861–1925) called his spiritual philosophy 'anthroposophy', meaning 'wisdom of the human being'. As a highly developed seer, he based his work on direct knowledge and perception of spiritual dimensions. He initiated a modern and universal 'science of spirit', accessible to anyone willing to exercise clear and unprejudiced thinking.

From his spiritual investigations Steiner provided suggestions for the renewal of many activities, including education (both general and special), agriculture, medicine, economics, architecture, science, philosophy, religion and the arts. Today there are thousands of schools, clinics, farms and other organizations involved in practical work based on his principles. His many published works feature his research into the spiritual nature of the human being, the evolution of the world and humanity, and methods of personal development. Steiner wrote some 30 books and delivered over 6000 lectures across Europe. In 1924 he founded the General Anthroposophical Society, which today has branches throughout the world.

THE EAST IN THE LIGHT OF THE WEST

The Children of Lucifer and the Brothers of Christ

RUDOLF STEINER

With a Foreword by Harry Collison

Nine lectures given in Munich between 23 and 31 August 1909

RUDOLF STEINER PRESS

Rudolf Steiner Press,
Hillside House, The Square
Forest Row, RH18 5ES

www.rudolfsteinerpress.com

Published by Rudolf Steiner Press 2017
First English edition published in 1922

Translated by S.M.K. Gandell and D.S. Osmond. This revised edition is
re-edited by Brendan McQuillan

Originally published in German under the title *Der Orient im Lichte des
Okzident, Die Kinder des Luzifer und die Brüder Christi* (volume 113 in the
Rudolf Steiner *Gesamtausgabe* or Collected Works) by Rudolf Steiner
Verlag, Dornach. Based on shorthand notes that were not reviewed or
revised by the speaker.

Published by kind permission of the Rudolf Steiner Nachlassverwaltung,
Dornach

A catalogue record for this book is available from the British Library

ISBN 978 1 85584 539 8

Cover by Morgan Creative
Typeset by DP Photosetting, Neath, West Glamorgan
Printed and bound by 4Edge Ltd., Essex

CONTENTS

FOREWORD

At Whitsuntide this year an international Congress of the Anthroposophical Movement was held at Vienna under the title of 'East and West'. Seventeen hundred people were present from all parts of Europe. It was an inspired gathering, held in a city where eastern and western elements have met and mingled for many centuries. Dr Steiner gave two courses of lectures, on Anthroposophy and Knowledge, and Anthroposophy and Sociology. The problem of East and West, spiritually considered, was the main theme. The Viennese public felt the message and gave him a great ovation, a sign that his lectures, with all their intensity of thought, had been appreciated and their impulse understood.

The Congress opened boldly with the clear statement that the problems of today are to be solved neither on economic nor on political platforms, but only on the basis of a new spiritual understanding, a creation of fresh spiritual values and ideals. Dr Steiner described the path of the soul to higher knowledge in ancient eastern methods—for example, in the yoga training—and he described how the ancient spirituality of the East was led to Europe by the civilization of ancient Greece. He showed how other elements of humanity in Northern and Western Europe, and later in America, had come into contact with this heritage from the ancient East and brought fresh faculties and impulses to bear on it. He claimed that anthroposophy points to a deeper knowledge, born of new faculties of spiritual perception, and is the only power great enough to draw together the conflicting elements in eastern and western points of view. Convincingly he showed how these seeds of new spiritual faculties are ready to burst into life in Europe and in the West, and how in this alone lies the solution of the world's problems today. If the West develops these latent spiritual faculties and so permeates her industrial and economic civilization with fresh spiritual values, the East will recognize her opportunity of a great spiritual revival and meet the West with understanding. Otherwise, despite all external appearances they will go on developing a latent hostility to our external western civilization.

Hence Dr Steiner claims that the keynote of the most immediate and practical problems of the hour lies in an understanding of the esoteric evolution of humanity, and of the relationship of man in East, Middle and West, in Past, Present and Future, to the spiritual worlds. The subject therefore that is dealt with esoterically in this book from a course of lectures given at private meetings of anthroposophical students twelve years ago has now become the most urgent and practical problem before the world. For, again and again, Dr Steiner has referred to the significant words of General Smuts, who said that the eyes of the world's statesmen must now be turned from the North Sea and the Atlantic to the Pacific, the immediate meeting-point of East and West.

Much will depend on a sufficient number of men and women realizing and understanding these problems in the light of the deeper knowledge that is contained, for example, in the course of lectures which has now been revised and made public, with Dr Steiner's permission, in this volume.

The translation of these lectures has been done chiefly by S.M.K. Gandell, who has already assisted me so greatly in former translations, and by Miss D. Osmond. I take this opportunity of conveying to them my sincere thanks for their cooperation in a very difficult task.

H. Collison
September 1922

LECTURE 1

Eternity and Time

23 August 1909

PATIENCE, or the ability to wait, is the inexorable demand in all departments of life. Failures are inevitable, and we must not grieve over them. Nature is not concerned over her countless failures, for the beings behind nature know that the higher spiritual law is bound to bring to pass the things which have been determined. Even so must students of anthroposophy learn to wait in faith for events which are to mature in the womb of time. And the central point of this faith, its firm foundation, is the symbol of the cross—as elucidated by a comprehension of the Christ principle. If we have come to know the reality of the Christ principle, we understand that this Christ principle is a force, a living force, and that it has been connected with human life on earth since the time that in the body of Jesus of Nazareth it united itself with one special human being. Since that time it has been with us, working among us, and we may become participators of its working if we endeavour to apply all means at our disposal to its understanding, in such a way that we make it the very life of our own souls.

When, however, we understand the Christ principle in this way, and know it to be in humanity, here on earth, and are able to come to it and draw water of life from the source, we then have the kind of belief which knows how to wait, not alone for everything which has to mature in the womb of time, but also for that which surely and certainly will mature for us human beings if we but have patience. When within this transitory existence we grasp the Christ principle, there will mature for us—in the womb of the transitory—the intransitory, the eternal, the immortal. Out of the womb of time, there is born for us human beings that which is beyond time. If we stand on this firm support, we base upon it, not a blind belief, but a belief permeated by wisdom, truth and knowledge, and we may say: What must, will come. And nothing prevents us from throwing our best energies into what we believe to be inevitable. Belief is the real fruit of the cross. It is that, which always calls out to us: 'Look at your failures, which seem to imply the death of your creative work; then look from your failures to the cross, and remember that on the cross hung the source of boundless eternal life which defeats death not only for itself but for all mankind.' From belief spring courage and perseverance. But courage, perseverance and belief alone are not sufficient; another necessary factor will have to be established more and more the further we progress towards the future, and must form an increasing part of everything that may be achieved for the future of humanity. And this is that we must become capable of never being confused about an idea when once we have recognized its correctness. We may have to admit a thousand times that it cannot be realized immediately, that we must wait in patience and without faltering, though we believe that the Christ force is working in the unfolding life of humanity in a way which will bring everything to birth at the right moment in the womb of time. We must, notwithstanding this, be able to judge of the rightness, of the indubitable rightness of the contents of our spiritual life. If we can wait for results, the occasions on which we have merely to wait when it is a question of deciding what is true, wise and right will become fewer and fewer. The cross alone gives vital courage and belief to our right understanding; but the star of the light-bearer, the star of Lucifer, if we surrender ourselves to it, can enlighten us every moment as to the rightness and the indubitableness of the spiritual ideas within us. That is the other centre of force on which we must take a firm stand; we must be capable of acquiring knowledge which goes into the depths of life, which goes behind the outer, material appearances, which sends its rays from the place where there is light, even when to human eyes and understanding all is dark. It was necessary for the progress of humanity that darkness should reign for a time, and the next lectures will show more and more clearly how necessary it was. This necessity is indicated in a profound way in the Gospel of St John. This darkness was illumined by what we call the Christ principle, the Christ.

A wonderfully beautiful legend tells us that when Lucifer fell from heaven to earth a precious stone fell from his crown. This precious stone—so the legend proceeds—became the vessel from which Christ Jesus took the holy Supper with His disciples; the same vessel received the Christ's blood when it flowed on the cross, and was brought by angels to the western world where it is received by those who wish to come to a true understanding of the Christ principle. Out of the stone, which fell from Lucifer's crown, was made the Holy Grail. This precious stone is in a certain respect nothing else—I will just mention it here, as the fact will be laid more plainly before your souls in the course of the next lectures—than the full power of the 'I'. In darkness this human 'I' had to be prepared for a new and more intelligent beholding of the radiance of Lucifer's star. This 'I' had to school itself by means of the Christ principle, it had to ripen by the aid of the stone fallen from Lucifer's crown, that is to say through anthroposophical wisdom, in order to become capable once more of bearing the light which comes not from without. This light, which only shines in us when we ourselves have the power to do what is requisite for acquiring it, must shine again in the world. Thus people who look at the future with full understanding know that anthroposophical work is work on the human 'I', which will make it into a vessel capable again of receiving the light which lives in a region where today our sight and intellect apprehend merely darkness and night. An old legend tells us that night was the original ruler. This night, however, is what today is filled with darkness. But if we permeate ourselves with the light which rises for us when we understand the Light-bearer, the other spirit Lucifer, then will our night be turned into day. Our eyes cannot see if the outer light does not illuminate the objects round us; our intellect fails if asked to penetrate beyond the outer nature of things. The star of Lucifer, however, which comes to us when clairvoyant investigation speaks, throws its light on what only seems to be night and changes it into day. And this also takes from us all deadening and paralysing doubt. Then we understand the cross of the Christ in the star of Lucifer. It may be said to be the mission of anthroposophical spiritual life for the future to give us on the one hand certainty and strength whereby, firmly rooted in spiritual life, we may become recipients of the light of the Light-bearer, and on the other hand to make us lean firmly on the rock of unquestioning conviction that nothing which is due to happen through the interaction of forces which are in the world shall fail to happen. Only through this twofold certainty shall we be able to accomplish what we have to do in the world; only through this twofold certainty shall we succeed in transplanting anthroposophy into life.

Therefore we must clearly recognize that we have not only the task of understanding the star of Lucifer, as it shone throughout human evolution till the precious stone fell out of Lucifer's crown, but that we have to receive this precious stone in its transformed character as the Holy Grail, that we must understand the cross in the star; we must know that we have to understand the luminous wisdom which shone in the world during primeval ages, and which we deeply revere as the wisdom of pre-Christian times. To this we must indeed look up in full devotion, and add to it that which could be given to the world through the mission of the cross. Not the least fraction of pre-Christian wisdom, of the light of the East, must be lost to us. We look up to Phosphoros, the Light-bearer, and indeed we revere this Light-bearer as the being through which alone we learn to understand the whole of the deep, inner meaning of the Christ. But side by side with Phosphoros we see Christophoros, the Christ-bearer, and we try to conceive of the mission of anthroposophy in such a way that it only can be fulfilled if the symbols of these two worlds really 'unite themselves in love'. If this is our conception of the mission of anthroposophy, Lucifer will guide us to the safety of a luminous spiritual life, and the Christ will guide us to the inner warmth of the soul which trusts and believes that that will come about which may be called the birth of the Eternal out of the Temporal.

And we shall further recognize that there is a light of the West that shines in order to make that which originates in the East more luminous than it is through its own power. A thing becomes luminous through the light by which it is illuminated. Therefore let no one say that any falsification whatever of eastern wisdom takes place when the light of the West shines on it. It will appear that what is beautiful and sublime seems most beautiful and sublime when illuminated by the noblest light. If we feel this idea and receive it into our souls, letting it fill them, we shall be able to learn in small things, through feeling and realization, what will come to pass in great matters. We shall say: We stand firmly rooted in our truths and wait patiently for their realization, however long deferred it may be.

Thus we work from one point of time to another in the firm belief that if we comprehend our mission rightly, we are working for that for which man ought to work, for eternity. For as far as human work is concerned, Eternity is the birth of that which has matured in Time.

LECTURE 2

Comparison of the Wisdom of East and West

24 August 1909

In this and the succeeding lectures we shall make it a special point to consider the wisdom of the eastern world, that is to say humanity's treasures of ancient wisdom in general, in the light which may be kindled by the knowledge of the Christ impulse and all that the course of the centuries has gradually evolved from this Christ impulse in the form of the wisdom of the western world. If anthroposophy is to be a living thing it must not consist in views and opinions of the higher worlds which are already in existence, taken from history and then taught, but it must comprise all the knowledge obtainable by us today about the nature of the higher worlds. Not only in olden times were there people who could turn their gaze towards these higher worlds and see them in the same way as we see the outer world with our physical eyes and understand it with our intellect. There have been such people at all periods of human evolution and there are such today. Humanity never has been dependent on the mere study of truths recorded in history, nor is man dependent on receiving these teachings about the higher worlds from any special physical place. Everywhere in the world the current of higher wisdom and knowledge may be tapped. It would be no wiser for our schools to teach mathematics or geography today by means of old documents, written in ancient times, than it is for us when studying the great wisdom of the supersensible worlds to consider only ancient, historical accounts. Therefore it will be our present task to approach the things of the higher worlds, the beings of the supersensible regions themselves, to review many things that are known, less known or quite unknown about these higher worlds, and then to ask ourselves what the people of older and of ancient times had to say about these things. In other words, we shall allow western wisdom to pass before our souls, and then enquire how that which we learn to know as western wisdom accords with what we may learn to know as eastern wisdom. The point is that the wisdom of the supersensible worlds, if related to man, may be grasped by the intellect. It has often been emphasized by me that any unprejudiced mind may grasp and comprehend the facts of the higher worlds. Although this unprejudiced common sense is a very rare faculty in our present time it does exist, and whoever is willing to exercise it can understand everything of the result of clairvoyant investigation that is related. It is true that these facts of the higher worlds can only be collected and investigated by so-called clairvoyant research, through the ascent into the higher worlds of people who have prepared themselves for this special purpose. And as in these higher worlds beings live which, in relation to man, we may call spirits or gods, the investigation of the higher worlds is in reality an association of the clairvoyant or the initiate with spirits or gods. Consequently a clairvoyant can only investigate the higher worlds by ascending the stages which lead to intercourse with the spirits or gods.

Much already has been said about these things at different times and places, and only the most essential part is here repeated. The first requisite for a person who wants to become clairvoyant in order to penetrate the higher worlds is nothing less than the acquisition of the faculty of seeing, knowing and experiencing without the help of the outer senses, not only without the help of instruments which have been built into our body such as eyes and ears, etc., but also unaided by the instrument which more especially serves our intellect, namely our mind. No more than we can see the supersensible worlds with physical eyes, or hear in them with physical ears, can we learn to know them through the intellect, which is bound up with our physical brain. Thus man has to become independent of the activity which he exercises when using his physical senses and his physical brain.

Now we know already that in normal human life there is a condition in which man is outside the instrument of his physical body, namely the condition of sleep. We know that of the four principles of human nature, the physical body, the etheric body, the astral body and the 'I' the latter two, the astral body and the 'I', gain a certain independence during sleep. During our waking life, from morning till we fall asleep at night, they are closely connected with the other two principles, with the physical and etheric bodies. But when we are asleep these four principles separate in such a way that the physical body with the etheric body remain lying on the bed, and the astral body and the 'I' are liberated and live in another world. Thus in the normal course of his life man is for some hours out of every 24 in a condition in which he is free from the instruments which are built into his physical body. But he has to pay for this liberation from his sense-body in a certain way with darkness; he cannot perceive the world in which he lives during sleep.

The organs and instruments necessary for man when he wishes to see in the spiritual world, in which he lives with his 'I' and his astral body at night, must of course be built into his astral body—relatively speaking into his 'I'. And the difference between a normal person of our time and a clairvoyant investigator consists in the fact that the astral body and the 'I' of the normal person are in a certain way unorganized and lacking organs of perception when they withdraw from the physical and etheric bodies at night, while in the astral body and 'I' of the clairvoyant investigator organs have been similarly developed to the eyes and ears of the physical body, though the organs are of a different kind. Thus the first task which the person who wants to become a clairvoyant investigator has to undertake is that of building into his hitherto unorganized astral body, and 'I' spiritual eyes, spiritual ears, etc., and of doing all that is necessary to develop these spiritual organs. But that is not the only thing necessary. Let us suppose that a person has progressed so far that, by the methods, which we shall presently mention, he has equipped his astral body and 'I' with spiritual eyes and ears, etc. Such a person would then have an astral body different from that of an ordinary person since he would have an organized astral body. He would, however, not yet be able to see in the spiritual world, or at any rate he would not be able to reach certain stages of seeing. Therefore something more is necessary. If in our present conditions man really wishes to ascend to conscious clairvoyance, it is not only necessary for spiritual eyes and ears to be developed in his astral body, but also for all that is thus plastically formed in this astral body to be imprinted upon the etheric body, even as a seal is stamped on sealing wax. Real, conscious clairvoyance begins when the organs, the spiritual eyes and ears, etc. formed in the astral body imprint themselves on the etheric body.

Thus the etheric body has to help the astral body and the 'I' if clairvoyance is to be brought about. Or in other words, all the principles of man's nature that we possess—the 'I', astral body and etheric body, with the sole exception of the physical body, have to work together to this end. Now there are greater difficulties for the etheric body than for the astral body in this respect. For the astral body and 'I' are, we might say, in the fortunate position of being free from the physical body once every 24 hours. From morning when we wake till evening when we go to sleep they are united with the physical body, and all that time the astral body and the 'I' are bound up with the forces of the physical body, which prevent the astral body and 'I' from developing their own organs. The astral body and 'I' are delicate soul-beings; they follow, by their own elasticity, the forces of the physical body, conforming themselves to it and taking on its form. Therefore at night the astral body and 'I' of normal persons still have these forces of the physical body within themselves as after-effects, and only by special measures can we free the astral body and 'I' from these after-effects and enable the astral body to develop its own form, that is to say its spiritual eyes and ears, etc. But we are at least in the fortunate position of having the astral body free in the course of every 24 hours; that is to say we have the possibility of working on it in such a way that it no longer follows the elasticity of the physical body at night but its own elasticity.

The preparatory exercises taken up by the clairvoyant investigator consist essentially in spiritual activities performed during waking life, which strongly influence the astral body and the 'I', and which have such strong inner effects that when at the moment of falling asleep the astral body and 'I' withdraw from the physical and etheric bodies they experience the after-effect of what has been done by way of special preparation for clairvoyant research.

Let us now consider two cases. The ordinary person living a normal life surrenders himself from morning till evening to the impressions of the outer world, which works on the outer senses and the intellect. He falls asleep at night, his astral body goes out of his physical body and is then given over entirely to the experiences of the day, following the elasticity of the physical body but not its own. But when through meditation, concentration and other exercises given to those who wish to tread the path to higher knowledge a person strongly influences his soul, that is his astral body and 'I', during waking life—in other words, when he has certain moments which he sets apart from ordinary daily life and in which he does something entirely different from the pursuits of ordinary waking life, and when in these particular moments he does not surrender himself to what the outer

world has to say to the senses and to the intellect, but to what
is a revelation from and a product of the spiritual worlds—a
marked change takes place. When an individual surrenders
himself to such things, when he spends part of his daily
waking life in meditation, concentration and other exercises,
for however short a time it may be, they affect his soul so
strongly that the astral body experiences the effects of this
meditation, concentration, etc. at night when it leaves the
physical body, and follows an elasticity different from that of
the physical body. The method for the attainment of clairvoyant powers employed by the teachers of this research is
drawn from the knowledge which has been tested for thousands of years in the way of exercises, meditation and concentration, which have to be followed in waking life in order
that they may have after-effects in sleeping life and produce a
different organization of the astral body. It is a great
responsibility which the person who gives such exercises to
his fellows takes upon himself. Such exercises are not
invented; they are the result of spiritual labour in the mysteries, in the occult schools. It is known that that which is
prescribed in these exercises works on the soul in such a way
that when this soul withdraws from the physical body in sleep
it develops its spiritual eyes and ears and its spiritual thinking
in the right way. If something wrong is done, or wrong
exercises are practised, certain results also follow. Effects do
not fail to appear, but in this case abnormal forms (or if we
want to use an expression of the sense world we might say
'unnatural' forms) are built into the astral body. What is the
meaning of unnatural forms being built into the astral body?
It means that forms are built into it that contradict the great
universe, that do not harmonize with it. It would correspond
in this sphere to building organs in our physical body which
could not hear outer sounds in the right way or see the outer
light in the right way, and which would not be in accord with
the outer world. Through wrong meditation and con-

centration man would therefore be brought into a position of contradiction to the universe, with regard to his astral body and his 'I'; and he would, instead of receiving organs through which the spiritual world could gradually reveal itself, be shattered by the influences of the spiritual world. He would experience these influences of the spiritual world not as something which benefited and enriched him, but as something which shattered his life and, if the methods were quite wrong, tore his being asunder.

It is important to take particular notice that we are here confronted with the fact that something which exists in the outer world—and we speak now of the spiritual outer world—may be beneficial to man in the highest degree, as well as harmful in the highest degree, according to the way in which he brings his own being to meet it. Let us suppose that a man with a wrongly developed astral body exposes himself to the spiritual world around him. This world works in upon him. Whereas this spiritual world would flow in on him and enrich him with the mysteries if he has cultivated his organs in the right way, it will tear him asunder and shatter him if he has developed them in the wrong way. It is one and the same outer world which in one case carries man upwards to the highest, in the other case shatters and ruins him—the same external world of which he will say that it is a divine and beneficent world when he carries within himself the right organs of perception, and a world of ruin and destruction when he has within himself an inner being which is not developed in the right way. In these words lies much of the key to an understanding of good and evil, of what is fruitful and what is destructive in the world. And this should enable us to see that the effect which any kind of beings of the outer world have on us is no standard by which to judge these beings themselves. According to the way in which we confront the outer world, the same being may either be beneficial or destructive to us, god or devil to our inner organization, and it is therefore imperative to bear this continually in mind.

We have now placed before our minds what the preparation for clairvoyant investigation is like with regard to our astral body and 'I'. And we have emphasized that we human beings are in a certain respect in a fortunate position, because we have our delicate astral body and 'I' outside our physical and etheric bodies for at least a certain time during each 24 hours. But the etheric body does not leave the physical body at night; it remains united with it. We know that not till the moment of death is the physical body deserted by the etheric body, which then withdraws along with the astral body and the 'I'. We need not mention today what becomes of these three principles of human nature between death and a new birth; we will only clearly present to our minds the fact that at death man is set free from his physical body and from all that is built into this physical body, free from the physical sense organs and free from the brain, the instrument of the intellect which works physically. The 'I', the astral body and the etheric body are then united in an appropriate fashion and can work together. Therefore it is the case that from the moment of death true clairvoyance sets in with regard to the previous life, although this at first lasts only for a short time. This has been often stated. Such a cooperation as normally only takes place at the moment of death must be made possible to the 'I', the astral body and the etheric body during life if complete clairvoyance is to be brought about. The etheric body must be liberated from the condition in which it is imprisoned during normal life; it must arrive at being able to use its elasticity and to become independent of the elasticity of the physical body, as the astral body is at night. For this purpose more intense, more strenuous and in a certain respect higher exercises are required. All these things will be mentioned again in their corresponding connection in the course of the next lectures. For the present it will suffice to

understand that such exercises are necessary, and that it is
not sufficient to have practised the preparatory exercises
which have the effect of developing spiritual eyes and ears in
the astral body, but that exercises for giving the etheric body
independence and freedom from the physical body are also
required. Just now, however, we will only consider the result.
It is not difficult to imagine from what has been said what this
result must be. In normal cases it is only at the moment of
death that the astral body and the etheric body can work
together free from the physical body. So if clairvoyance is to
be aroused, something must take place which can only be
compared with what sets in for man at the moment of death.
That is to say, man must, if he wishes to become consciously
clairvoyant, reach a stage of development where he is just as
independent of his physical body and the use of the members
of his physical body during life as he is at the moment of
death.

By what means can man acquire such independence from
his physical body, and bring himself into a condition which
resembles the moment of physical death? Only by cultivating
certain feelings and shades of feeling which stir the soul so
forcibly that by their power they seize the etheric body and lift
it out of the physical body. Such strong impulses of thought,
feeling and will must work in the soul that an inner force is
aroused which frees the etheric body from the physical body,
at any rate for certain moments. In these moments, however,
the physical body must absolutely be as if dead to ordinary,
normal human life. But this cannot be brought about by
external, physical methods in our period of human evolution.
Anyone who thinks that such things can be brought about by
physical methods would become the victim of a stupendous
delusion. Such a person would wish to enter the spiritual
worlds by adhering to the methods of the physical world; that
is to say he would not yet have attained to a real belief in the
force of the spiritual worlds. For purely subjective experi-

ences, impulses proceeding from the strong, energetic life of the soul are alone competent to bring about this deathlike condition. And speaking in the abstract, we may say for the present that the most essential thing for bringing about such a condition is that man experiences a change, as it were, a turning upside down of his sphere of interests. For ordinary life provides man with certain interests. These interests play their part from morning till night. Man is interested and quite rightly, for he must live in the world—in things that appeal to his eyes, his ears, his physical intellect, his physical feelings, etc. He is interested in what confronts him in the outer world. One thing interests him more, another less; he pays more attention to one thing and less to another, and that is natural. In these fluctuating interests, binding him to the tapestry of the outer world by a certain power of attraction, man lives, and by far the greater part of our present humanity lives in these interests alone. Nevertheless it is possible for man, without detriment to the freshness and intensity of these interests, to bring about moments in his life in which these outer interests are not at all active, in which, if we wish to express it radically, this whole outer sense world becomes absolutely indifferent to him, in which he kills out absolutely all the interest forces which fetter him to this or that object in the world of the senses. It would be wrong for a man not to reserve this deadening of his interests in the outer world for certain 'festival moments' in life, it would be wrong to extend it over his whole life. He would then become incapable of taking part in the work of the outer world, whereas we are called to take part in the outer world and in its life.

We must therefore reserve for 'times of high festival' this possibility of letting all interests in the surrounding world die out; we must, so to say, acquire this twofold nature. On the one hand we must feel a fresh and vital interest in everything which goes on in the outer world in the way of joy and sorrow, of pleasure and pain, and of life which is blossoming and flourishing and of life which is dying. This freshness and originality of our interest in the outer world must be kept alive in our earthly life; we must not become strangers upon earth, for then we should act from egoism and deprive the stage to which our forces must be devoted in our present evolution of these forces. But on the other hand we must, if we wish to ascend into the higher worlds, cultivate the other side of our being, which consists in killing out during 'moments of Holy Day' all our interests in the outer world, of letting them die out. And if we have patience and persever-ance and energy and strength to practise this as long and as much as our karma demands, this deadening of interest in the outer world at last liberates a strong energetic force in our inner being, because that which we kill out in this way in the outer world reappears as higher and more abundant life in the inner world. We experience an entirely new kind of life; we experience the moment in which we can say: That which we can see with our eyes and hear with our ears is only a small part of life. There is an entirely different life, life in the spiritual world; a resurrection in the spiritual world, a transcending of what we usually call life, a transcending in such a way that not death but a higher life is the result. As soon as this pure spiritual force has grown strong enough in our inner being, we may gradually experience moments in which we become rulers and lords over our etheric body, when this etheric body does not take on the shape forced upon it by the elasticity of the lungs and the liver, but the shape forced upon it from above downwards by our astral body. Thus we imprint on our etheric body the shape which, through meditation, concentration, etc., we have first imprinted on our astral body. We imprint the plastic form of our astral body on the etheric body, and we ascend from 'preparation' to 'illumination'—the next stage of clairvoyant research. The first stage, by which our astral body is changed in such a way that it receives organs, is also called 'purification', because the astral body is purified and purged of the forces of the outer world, and conforms to the inner forces—purification, cleansing, catharsis. But the stage at which the astral body succeeds in imprinting its own form on the etheric body implies that in a spiritual sense light begins to shine around us, that the spiritual world around us is revealing itself and that 'illumination' is setting in.

What I have just described goes hand in hand with certain experiences which man goes through, with typical experiences which are the same for everyone, and which everyone who treads this path experiences the moment he is ripe for it, if he pays the necessary attention to certain things and occurrences which are beyond the physical. The first experience, which occurs through the organization of the astral body and which therefore comes about as an effect of meditation, concentration, etc., might be called an inner experience of the feelings describable as an inward division of the whole of our personality. The moment this is experienced one can say to oneself: Now you have become something like two personalities, you are like a sword in its scabbard. Formerly you might have compared yourself with a sword that does not lie loosely in its scabbard but is one with it, the two consisting of one; you felt yourself one with your physical body. But now you seem, although lying in your physical body like a sword in its scabbard, to be a being which feels itself to be something apart from the sheath of the physical body, in which it is lying. You feel yourself to be within the physical body, but not grown into one with it, not as if consisting of one piece with it. This inward liberation, this inward realization of oneself as a second personality that has emerged from the first, is the first great experience on the way to clairvoyant vision of the World. The fact must be emphasized that this first experience is an experience of the inner feelings. One must feel that one is lying within one's old personality, and yet feel free and mobile within it. The analogy with the sword and its scabbard is of course rough. For the sword feels itself cramped on all sides by the scabbard, while man, when he has this experience, has a strong feeling of inner mobility, as if he might break on all sides through the limits of his physical body, as if he could forsake it by falling through the skin of his physical body and stretch out his feelers far, far into a world which, although still dark, begins to be perceptible to his feeling in the darkness, one might say, begins to be knowable through inner touch. This is the first great experience man has.

The second great experience is that this second personality which now exists within the first gradually becomes capable of really leaving this first personality, of stepping out of it. This experience expresses itself in the fact that, although often only for a short time, one feels as if one could see oneself, as if one stood confronting oneself like a double. This is the second experience, and it is moreover of much greater importance than the first. With it something is connected which it is very difficult for man to bear. It must never be forgotten that in normal life man is contained within his physical body. That which lives within man's physical body as astral body and 'I' accommodates itself to the forces of the physical body: it yields as it were to them; it conforms itself to the bodily forces, assuming the shapes of the liver, the heart, the brain, etc. And this is also true of the etheric body, so long as it remains within the physical body. Now we all know what is indicated by the expression brain, heart, etc., what wonderful instruments and organs they are, how complete in themselves, how perfect as creations! What is all human art and human creative work compared with the creative work, the art and technique necessary for constructing such wonderful instruments as the heart, the brain, etc. What is everything that man can accomplish at the present stage of his evolution in the way of art and technical skill compared with that divine art and technique which have built up our physical body and which, therefore, also guard us as long as we are within it. So we are not merely in an abstract sense devoted to our physical bodies during daily life, but interwoven with a concrete creation of the gods. Our etheric and astral bodies are fitted into forms created by the gods. If we now become free and independent there will be a change. We free ourselves at the same time from a wonderful instrument of divine creation. Thus we do not leave the physical body as some imperfect thing to be looked down upon, but as the temple which the gods have built for us and in which normally we live during our waking life. Such a temple do we leave on abandoning the physical body. What are we then?

Let us suppose that at a certain moment we could leave this physical body without further preparation, let us suppose that some magician (of whatever kind he might be) could assist us to leave our physical body, and that our etheric body accompanied our astral body, and that we, in a certain respect, went through an experience comparable with the moment of death; let us suppose that we could do this without the preparation of which we have spoken. What should we be when, outside the physical body, we confront ourselves? We are then what in the course of the world evolution we have made of ourselves from incarnation to incarnation. As long as from morning to night we are within our physical body, this divine creation, the temple of our physical body, corrects what we have incorporated within ourselves in the course of our incarnations on earth. But the moment we step out of it, our astral and etheric bodies show what they have accumulated from incarnation to incarnation and appear as they are according to what they have made of themselves. If a man thus unprepared leaves his physical body, he is not a spiritual being of a higher, nobler and purer form than the form was which he had in his physical body, but a being laden with all the imperfections heaped up in his karma during his incarnations. All this remains invisible so long as the temple of our body encloses our etheric body, our astral body and our 'I'. It becomes visible the moment we step out of our physical body with the higher principles of our being. Then there appear before us, if at the same moment we become clairvoyant, all the inclinations and passions which still remain with us as the result of our former incarnations. In the course of the future evolution of our earth we have still to go through many incarnations, full of activities and accomplishment. The inclinations, instinct and passions for much that you will do later are already within you, developed through incarnations in former times. Everything that man is capable of accomplishing in the world in certain directions, all obligations to others incurred by offences against them for which reparation has to be made in the future, are already incorporated in the astral body and the etheric body when he leaves his physical body. We confront ourselves so to say naked as a soul being, if at the moment of leaving our body we are clairvoyant. That is to say, we stand before our spiritual vision in such a way that we know how much worse we are than would be the case if we had attained the perfection possessed by the gods, which made them capable of creating the wonderful building of our physical body. We perceive at this moment how far we are from the perfection which we must hold before us as our future ideal of development.

We know at this moment how deeply we have sunk below the world of perfection.

This is the experience which is connected with 'illumination'; it is the experience which is called the meeting with the Guardian of the Threshold. That which is real does not become more or less real according to our seeing or not seeing it. That shape which we see in the moment just described is always there, is always within us; but because we have not yet got loose from ourselves, because we do not confront ourselves but are within ourselves we do not see it.

In ordinary life, that which we see at the moment that clairvoyantly we step out of ourselves is the Guardian of the Threshold. He shields us from an experience that we must first learn to bear. We must first acquire a strong enough force to enable us to see a world of the future before us, and to look without fear and horror upon what we have become, because we know for certain that we can make it all right again. The capacity, which we must possess for experiencing this moment without being depressed by it, must be acquired during the preparation for clairvoyant investigation. This preparation consists, abstractly expressed, in making the active, positive qualities of our souls strong and energetic, in bringing our courage, our feeling of freedom, our love, our energy of thought and our energy of lucid intellect to the greatest possible height, so that we step out of our physical body not as weak people but as strong. If, however, there is too much left in man of what is called anxiety and fear, he will not be able to endure this experience of encountering the Guardian of the Threshold without harm.

Thus we see that there are certain conditions to be fulfilled before looking into the spiritual worlds, those worlds which in a certain respect hold out a prospect of the highest that we can think of for life in our present development of humanity, but at the same time demand of man a complete transformation of his being such as he has to attain in the solemn 'Holy Day moments' before mentioned. It is a real blessing in our present time for the aspirant, before he proceeds to this experience, to be told what those who have gained experience in the higher worlds have seen. We can understand even when we cannot see. But by making increasing efforts to reach an intellectual comprehension of what the clairvoyant tells us, and coming to the conclusion, after a survey of everything life brings us, that the clairvoyant's reports are quite sensible after all, we shall be doing the right thing at the present time. We must become anthroposophists before aspiring to clairvoyance, and we must learn to know anthroposophy thoroughly. If we do this, the great, comprehensive, strengthening, encouraging and refreshing ideas and thoughts of anthroposophy give to the soul not only a working hypothesis, but also qualities of feeling, will and thought, which make the soul like tempered steel. If the soul has gone through this process, the moment of meeting with the Guardian of the Threshold becomes something quite different from what it would have been otherwise. Fear and terror, states of anxiety and care, are conquered in quite a different way if previously we have learned to understand and to grasp what is related about the higher worlds. And later, when a person has had this experience, when he has confronted himself and thus has met the Guardian of the Threshold, the world begins to show itself to him in quite a different way. Everything in the world may be said to wear a new aspect. And a justifiable opinion might be expressed by the following illustrations. I had supposed up till now that I knew what fire is but that was only an illusion. For what I have called fire up till now would be like calling the tracks of a carriage on a road the only reality, and denying that a carriage in which a person was sitting must have been passing that way. I declare these tracks on the road to be the signs, the outer expression of the carriage which has passed there and in which a person was sitting. I have not seen the person who passed there, but he is the cause of these tracks, he is the reality. And a person who believed the marks left by the wheels to be something complete in themselves, something real and basic, would be taking the outer expression for the thing itself.

That which our senses see as flashing fire bears the same proportion to its reality, to the spiritual being which stands behind it, as do the tracks on the road to the person who was sitting in the carriage which passed there. In fire we have only an outer expression. Behind what our eyes see as fire and what we feel as heat is the real spiritual entity, which has only its outer expression in the outer fire. Behind what we inhale as air, behind what enters our eyes as light, and behind what our ears perceive as sound are active beings spiritual and divine, whose outer garments only we behold in fire, in water and in what surrounds us in the different realms of nature.

In the so-called secret teaching, in the teaching of the mysteries, the experience which is then gone through is called the passage through the elementary worlds. Whereas previously one had lived in the belief that what we know as fire is a reality, one then becomes aware that living beings are hidden behind the fire. We become, so to say, acquainted with fire, more or less intimately as something quite different from what it appears to be in the world of the senses. We become acquainted with the fire-beings, with what is the soul of the fire. Just as our souls are hidden behind our bodies, so the soul and spirit of the fire are hidden by the fire which we perceive with our outer senses. We penetrate into a spiritual domain when we experience the soul and spirit of fire in this way, and the experience by which we realize that the outer fire is no reality, that it is a mere illusion, a mere garment, and that we now move among the fire-gods just as we did formerly among people of the physical world, is called 'living in the element of fire', to use the terms of occult science. It is the same with that which we breathe. The moment that what we breathe as outer air becomes to us only the garment of the living beings within it, we live in the element of air. And so when one has passed through the meeting with the Guardian of the Threshold, that is to say, when one has acquired true self-knowledge, one can ascend to experiencing the beings in the so-called elements, in the elements of fire, of water, of air and of earth. These four classes of gods or spirits live a real existence in the elements, and a person who has reached the stage which has just been described is in touch with the divine spiritual beings of the elements. He lives in the elements; he experiences earth, water, air and fire. That which in ordinary life is designated by these words is only the outer garment, the outer expression of divine-spiritual beings behind it. It becomes plain, therefore, that certain spiritual divine beings live in that which meets us (speaking according to spiritual science) as solid matter or earth, as fluid matter or water, as volatile matter or air, and as warm, fiery matter or fire.

These, however, are not the highest spiritual beings. When we have struggled on through the experiences of the elementary world, we ascend to the entities which stand in the relation of creators towards the spirits who live in the elements. For let us consider our physical surroundings. We find that they consist of the four outer principles of the elementary world. Whether we take plants, or animals, or stones, or anything else on the physical plane, they consist according to spiritual science either of the solid element, that is earth, or the fluid element, water, or the gaseous element, air, or the fiery element, fire. Of these elements the things which physically surround us in the world of stones, of plants, of animals and of people are composed. And we know that behind what physically surrounds us there are, as creative and fructifying forces, those forces which for the most part come to us from the sun. We know that the sun calls forth budding and germinating life out of the earth. Thus the sun sends to the earth forces which—considered physically for the moment—make it possible for us to per-ceive on earth with our physical senses that which lives in fire, in air, in water and in earth. We see the sun physically because it radiates physical light. This physical light is sus-tained by physical matter. Man sees the sun from sunrise to sunset, and he does not see it when the physical earth sub-stance hides it; he does not see it from sunset to sunrise. In the spiritual world there is no such darkness as reigns in physical life from sunset to sunrise.

When the clairvoyant has gained what has been described,

when he perceives behind fire the spirits of fire, behind air the spirits of air, behind water the spirits of water, and behind earth the spirits of earth, in that moment he sees behind these divine spiritual beings their higher ruler, their higher Lord, the entity which in comparison to these beings of the elements is like the warming, illuminating beneficent sun as compared to the budding and germinating life on our earth. That is to say, the clairvoyant ascends from a contemplation of the elementary gods to the contemplation of those higher divine beings which in the spiritual world may be symbolically compared with the sun in its physical relation to the earth. Behind the beings of the elements a high spiritual world is seen, the spiritual sun. When for the clairvoyant that which otherwise is darkness becomes light, when he attains to clairvoyance, to 'illumination', he realizes the spiritual sun, that is to say the higher divine spiritual beings in the same way as the physical eye realizes the physical sun. And when does he penetrate to these higher divine spiritual beings? At the moment when, as it were, for other people the spiritual darkness is at its densest. When man's astral body and 'I' are free, that is to say, from the moment of falling asleep to that of waking, man lives surrounded by darkness because he does not see the spiritual world which then surrounds him. This darkness increases gradually, reaches its densest point and decreases again until the morning when he awakes. It comes, as it were, to a point in which it reaches its densest degree. This densest degree of spiritual darkness may be compared with what in outer life is called the hour of midnight. Just as normally the outer physical darkness is then at its densest, since it increases towards this moment and then decreases, so there is a densest degree of spiritual darkness, a midnight.

At a certain stage of clairvoyance it happens that the spirits of the elements are seen during the time when for other people the spiritual darkness begins to increase, and similarly during the time in which darkness decreases again. In other words, if only a lower stage of clairvoyance has been reached one experiences, so to say, certain gods of the elements, but just at the time of the highest spiritual moment, the midnight hour, darkness may still set in and 'illumination' only begins again after this moment has been passed. When, however, a definite stage of clairvoyance is reached, the midnight hour becomes so much the more 'illuminated'; and just at this midnight-hour, at the time when the normal person is, so to say, most shut off from the divine-spiritual world, most entangled in maya, or illusion, one ascends into the light. At this time one beholds those spiritual beings which, compared to the gods of the elements, are like the sun compared to the physical earth. One beholds the higher creative gods, the sun gods, in the moment which is technically called 'beholding the sun at midnight'.

These are the stages which today, as at all times, have to be lived through by those who wish to work themselves up to clairvoyant investigation, who wish to look through the veil which in the shape of the earthly elements is drawn over the real world. They are: the feeling of freedom inside one's ordinary personality, like that of a sword in its sheath; the feeling of being outside the physical body, as if the sword were drawn out of its sheath; the meeting with the Guardian of the Threshold; experiencing the gods of the elements, that is, experiencing the great moment when the beings of fire, air, water and earth become beings among whom we walk and with whom we associate as in ordinary life we associate with human beings; and lastly, experiencing the moment when we behold the king, the commander, the leader of these beings of the elements. These are the stages which could be experienced at all past times and which can still be experienced today. These are the stages (already often described, for they can be described in many ways, and still the description always remains imperfect) leading upwards into the spiritual worlds. We were obliged to present them to our souls so as to see what man at all times has had to do himself, in order to learn to know the divine-spiritual beings. And we shall further have to place before our souls what it is which man experiences in these divine-spiritual worlds; we shall have to realize some of the more concrete preparations to be gone through in order to meet the gods. And when we have presented this to our souls and the way in which it can be attained by western initiation, we shall compare what we have thus gained with what has been given to humanity in the way of oriental tradition and ancient wisdom. And in making this comparison, we shall be shedding the light of the Christ upon the wisdom of pre-Christian times.

LECTURE 3

The Nature of the Physical and the Astral Worlds

25 August 1909

Our attention has been called to the fact that to human beings at a certain stage of evolution, the external phenomena of warmth, air, water, etc. become living and permeated with spirit, and it has been said that this stage may be designated as that of 'penetration into the world of spirits of the elements'. I would ask those who have been students of spiritual science for some time to note the words carefully, and to realize that they are used not in an approximate but in an exact sense. 'Spirits of the elements' was the expression I used, and not 'elementary spirits'.

It must be pointed out that when we ascend into supersensible realms, other worlds, two of which shall be named, are added to the ordinary world which is experienced by means of the sense organs: They are to be found behind what is perceptible by the senses and comprehensible to the intellect. There are certain striking characteristics which give an idea of the difference between our world and the two higher ones adjoining it. The first region hidden behind our ordinary world is named, as everyone knows, the astral or soul world; the other, the spiritual world, is still more deeply hidden. In the physical world one of the most comprehensive laws is that of growth and decay, of coming into being and passing away. Look where we will in the physical world we find that a characteristic of its highest beings is that they are born and that they die within it; the inanimate kingdom of the minerals, belonging to the lower realms of nature, may arouse an illusion of permanence within the physical world, but if the mineral king-dom be observed over long periods of time the law of growth and decay is found there.

Observation of the astral world, however, reveals the fact that here the capacity of transformation or metamorphosis is as predominant as is the law of birth and decay in the physical world. In the astral world we have to do with moving images changing one into the other, in a state of perpetual meta-morphosis. Even the astral body of man— which of all astral phenomena is the most intimately bound up with us, visible to the seer as a kind of aura or cloudlike formation around the physical body—shares this characteristic of continual trans-formation. That which envelopes and penetrates the human being in the form of an astral auric cloud changes practically every moment as higher or lower impulses develop in him, as he experiences wilder or calmer passions, or cultivates thoughts of different nature according to the character of the will impulses. Images and shapes arise in the astral auric cloud, and as different thoughts rise and fade away its colour and form may continually change. There is, however, a certain fundamental character and colour in the astral aura of every individual, corresponding to his more or less perma-nent type of character. Self-metamorphosis, then, is of the very nature of the human astral body. We have seen that the beings visible to a man in the astral world after he has reached the stage of illumination meet him as good or as evil beings according to his own preparation. So strong is the capacity of metamorphosis in those beings, which are invisible on the physical plane and only perceptible in the astral and higher worlds, that they may change from good into evil, from light into dark.

In the real spiritual world there is permanence, even if it is relative. For this reason the inner being of man, if it is to exist without a break from one incarnation to another, must pass through the spiritual worlds, because only there is to be found a certain—not external—but relative permanence or continuity.

The rhythm of growth and decay is the predominant characteristic of the physical world, metamorphosis from one form to another of the astral world, permanence or continuity of the spiritual world. First we must realize that the materials for the building up of the human being have been obtained from these worlds; man has been constructed out of them. The physical world lies before him; the other worlds open up to him through initiation—through preparation and development of supersensible faculties of perception. Man then first learns to know what is hidden from him in the ordinary world, but what has just as real an existence. When in ordinary life an outer sheath or expression of some being is found, as for example fire or air, the being itself is to be sought in a higher world. In order to meet the beings whose expression is physical fire, man must ascend to a region higher than the physical world. That which is the cause and origin of fire, for instance, can only be discovered by rising from the physical plane to the world above it, because the beings in question send down an expression of themselves into the lower world but remain as to their essential nature in the higher region. This holds good not only for external phenomena such as fire, air, water or earth, but also for everything living within us in the physical world. Our feelings, perceptions and thoughts exist in the physical world along with phenomena of colour, sound, tastes, scent, etc. It must be clear to us that everything which constitutes man in an incarnation, every feeling experienced between birth and death, every thought, every idea, is a phenomenon of the physical world. And spiritual beings live behind our feelings and the whole of our soul life just as they do behind the external phenomena of colour, sound, scent or, as we say in spiritual science, behind fire, air, water and so on. In the same way, the 'I', the self within the physical world, is not our real being, is not what is called our Higher Self, for that is to be found in a supersensible world behind our feelings and sensations. This Higher Self is experienced in a true sense only by attaining to supersensible worlds, where it manifests itself in quite another form.

I will show you by a definite example the relation of the self of man living in the physical world to the Higher Self; this example holds good for present conditions of life only, since anyone who has spiritual sight knows that the nature of these things changes in the course of time. Let us suppose that an individual has done an injustice to another and experiences the pang of conscience. I refer here to those special psychic experiences usually expressed by the word conscience. In ordinary life, conscience is a term used of certain inner voices demanding that we should set right any wrong we may have committed. Most people hardly ever come to the point of thinking about the nature of conscience; they recognize as a kind of vague feeling that an injustice should be righted—the soul is uneasy when this has not been done. For human beings in the physical world conscience is an inner experience of the soul. The spiritual Seer, however, observing from the astral world the person who has done the act of injustice, sees the pang of conscience surrounding him in remarkable astral shapes—shapes which are absent if no pang of conscience has been felt. The origin of these forms may be explained as follows. Suppose somebody has done an injustice: from thoughts which have led to the unjust act other thought-forms develop as the metamorphosis of the first. Everything that a person thinks and feels exists in his astral aura as a form or shape of the nature of thought or of feeling. A thought which is, let us say, distinct, definite, can be seen in sharp outline hovering round a person, and wild thoughts or passions in confused outlines. At the time when a person is doing an injustice he has certain thoughts and feelings; these forms detach themselves from him and live in his environment, but the essential point is that they do not remain in this condition but draw nourishment from certain worlds. Just as the wind rushes into empty spaces, beings from definite regions (of which more later) rush into the forms created by the pang of conscience and fill them with living substance. Thus in his own thought-forms a person offers opportunity for other beings to live in his environment, and these beings are really the cause of the sting of conscience. If the beings were not present the conscience would not sting. When a person begins to feel these beings unconsciously, the first gnawing of an uneasy conscience is experienced.

This example shows us that spiritual sight reveals a reality very different from that presented to physical sight. If a person is to contact the spirits of conscience, who live upon the astral plane, he must look through his conscience into the higher worlds in the same way as would be necessary in order to perceive the spiritual beings who animate physical life.

From different lectures we know that the human soul has changed in the course of long periods of time—human consciousness of today is different from the consciousness, let us say, of the ancient Indian people in the first post-Atlantean epoch, and it in its turn was very different from the consciousness of the Atlantean age. The clear waking consciousness of the physical world has developed from a dim, primitive clairvoyance. The farther we go back in evolution, the more traces do we find of this primitive clairvoyance.

We need not go further than some thousands of years, and we shall find that many people were then able not merely to perceive physical fire but to look through it to the spirits of the element of fire. Gradually it came about that the higher world withdrew from human consciousness and the latter came to be limited to the physical world. This holds good not merely for the external sense world, but for the whole of the life of the soul in the physical world. So it is stated that in a phenomenon like conscience a modern spiritual seer perceives astral forms around human beings, and the ancestors of this modern man, being endowed with clairvoyance, must have been able to see these astral forms. Just as fire conceals the spirits of the fire, so does human conscience—the inner voice—conceal the world of the spirits of conscience. The astral phenomena must have been perceptible to men of ancient times; but they could at that time have had no inner conscience, since it had not yet developed. What we of today call the psychological phenomenon of conscience was not present in our forefathers, but on the other hand they could see in the astral aura what is now only perceptible to the eye of the seer; modern people feel the inner voice of conscience and the spirits of conscience are hidden behind it.

I have brought forward this example deliberately, because it affords concrete evidence of these matters. It is possible to indicate precisely the epoch in external history when the transition took place from perception of the outer spirits of conscience to the awakening of conscience as an inner voice. Compare the Orestes of Aeschylus with the same theme as treated by Euripides, who lived a short while later. Between the age of Aeschylus and that of Euripides—a few years only—occurred the transition which confirms what I have just said. In the story of Orestes as related by Aeschylus, Agamemnon returns home after the war and is murdered by his unfaithful wife. His son, Orestes, who is absent, returns and takes vengeance upon his mother for the death of his father, because one of the gods demands that he shall do so; his act is in harmony with the national feeling of those times that declares that his act is righteous and that he has done his duty. But as the result of the murder of his mother, Orestes sees the Erinyes, the avenging goddesses, approaching. These avenging goddesses of Greek mythology are simply a pictorial image of what has just been described as a reality for spiritual perception. And now let us see whether in this old drama there is any phenomenon which could be described by the modern word conscience. There is not even a word for it in any ancient language, as research would testify. In the poem of Euripides who used the same story a few decades later, we find no Furies, no avenging goddesses; there people hear instead the inner voice of conscience. Concretely perceptible, in the interval between the lives of these two poets, conscience arose. Clairvoyance was so vivid and real in human evolution before this age that the feeling experienced by man, as the result of an unrighteous act, was entirely different from what it became later. Man's clairvoyant vision was still open; he saw in his environment what I have described in the Greek as the Erinyes. The inner feeling which he experienced in the presence of this vision was one in accordance with the character of the astral world he wanted to change, to transform the images surrounding him. As soon as an unrighteous or unjust deed has been wiped out by turning it into a good one, the Erinyes change into the beneficent Eumenides. Man felt that an evil deed caused a terrible result in the astral world, that it must be transformed, and that by a positive act he must bring about its metamorphosis. His actions then were in accordance with what he saw in his environment. The inner voice of conscience was nonexistent.

Everything in the world and in the inner life of the soul as well has developed or evolved, conscience among the rest. If anyone were to go back some thousands of years in search of an instance of our modern soul life, he would make a great mistake. For transitions such as this take place with considerable suddenness. Just as in the plant there is a sudden metamorphosis from leaf to flower, so does this occur in spiritual evolution. The phrase 'nature makes no jumps' is untrue; nature continually makes jumps at decisive moments. And such sudden transitions are perceptible in spiritual life. For centuries and millennia there is slow and gradual development; but then there is a sudden change, as in the case of the conscience in the fifth century BC where an earlier tragic poet makes no mention of conscience in his dramas and only a few decades afterwards it is introduced for the first time. With this is connected the fact that clairvoyant perception of the spirits of conscience, the Erinyes, has disappeared. The spiritual beings are of such a nature that our inner experience of conscience comes between us and them in the same way as the outer expression of fire hides the spirits of the element of fire.

This points to the fact that so far as the physical world is concerned, limits of experience are set in two directions. The outer phenomena of the senses, colour, form, and so on, form the boundary at which the external spirits are to be found. But behind the inner phenomena of conscience, memory, feeling, will and thought, a spiritual element exists as it does behind fire, air, water or earth. The spirit is hidden behind them. When conscience came to be a voice speaking in the human soul, it interposed itself in front of the world of the Furies and hid that from human sight. The historical life of humanity becomes intelligible only when considered from this inner point of view. Mankind can understand nothing of what has come to pass in the world if it leaves spiritual facts out of sight in considering evolution or becoming.

We may now ask, what is the relation of the inner and the outer spiritual realms to each other? We know that man as a fourfold being is composed of physical, etheric, astral bodies and 'I', and that this fourfold constitution is to be traced back to the very source and origin of humanity. Man did not originate on the earth, for the earth itself has passed through other embodiments, that of Saturn, of Old Sun and Old Moon. The first germ of the physical body of man arose on the Saturn embodiment, the etheric body was added on the Old Sun, and the astral body on the Old Moon. The 'I' was first incorporated into this threefold constitution on the Earth. Evolution is by no means such a simple matter as to involve merely a transition from the Saturn embodiment into the Old Sun, thence into Old Moon and thence again into Earth; the process is much more complicated than that. Even if we speak of the transition from Saturn to Old Sun and of this to Old Moon, we could not speak thus simply of the Old Moon evolution itself. I have said that during the Old Moon evolution there was a separation of moon and sun. Whereas the Saturn and Old Sun embodiments may perhaps be spoken of as single bodies, during the Old Moon two bodies emerged from the one, producing moon and sun, which then existed at the same time. These two bodies then united again after a time, passed through an intermediate condition and arose later as the Earth embodiment. During the earliest period of this Earth evolution, the substances and beings now to be found in our present sun and moon were united with the earth; our present sun beings then separated from earth, which remained for a time in connection with, but later separated off from, our present moon; after the separation of the moon, the earth remained alone, between the moon and the sun. These three bodies were one in the beginning; only later did first the sun and then the moon develop out of the earth.

Let us now enquire as to the spiritual meaning of this separation; we will leave out of consideration the first separation occurring during the Old Moon period and look at what happened in this connection during the Earth period. Certain beings pass through their evolution on the earth, while the sun and the moon afford evolutionary opportunities to others. Beings at a different stage of development from that of man separated from the earth with the sun, because their evolution could not proceed otherwise. At the time, therefore, of the separation of the sun from the earth, we are faced with the fact that man was left behind, since the nature of his evolution demanded the conditions afforded by the earth. The other beings, whose evolution could not proceed upon the earth, separated from the earth the substances necessary for them, and built their sun abode. From there they influence and work upon the earth. In physical sunbeams, as they lighten and warm the earth, we see the streaming activities of the sun spirits; the sunbeams are the outer, corporal manifestation of sun beings. That is the meaning of the separation of the sun from the earth.

What was the meaning of the separation of the moon? Man could not have kept pace with the evolutionary tempo of the sun beings if the sun beings had remained in union with the earth. The evolutionary tempo of the earth was slowed down by the separation of the sun, but still it was not suitable for human beings—it was too slow. If the moon had remained in connection with the earth, man would have become hardened or mummified. The earth would gradually have become a planetary body from which human beings would have developed with forms like dead bodies that lack inner spiritual and psychic life. The moon had to withdraw from the earth in order that the right evolutionary tempo for the being of man might be set up. If the sun had remained with the earth, man would have been forced into an outer life and activity which he could not have endured; if the moon had remained he would have become impervious to stimulus, he would have dried up, lacking vital force. The stimulus received by man from the sun was an external one which would have produced too rapid a tempo. In the same way as the sun stimulates the life of the flowers in the fields, man's thoughts, feelings and will would have been stimulated from without, but at such a rate that he would have been burnt up by physical and spiritual sun fire. The source of this stimulus departed from the earth and in this way its influence was weakened. At first, because of the hardening tendency inherent in the earth, the sun's influence had too little effect, and a portion of these hardening factors had to leave with the moon. Therewith came into the evolution of Earth and of man a new vitalizing principle, the stimulating influence of which was exactly in the opposite way to that of the sun from without. The new stimulus came from within. The life of the soul in the physical world could develop only because man was saved from this hardening and mummification by withdrawal of the moon.

Ask someone whose spiritual sight is able to penetrate into the cosmos as to the origin of man's perception of the external world and his answer will be that it is to be found in the physical or spiritual sun elements. Ask what lies at the basis of inner experience, of thought, of feeling, of conscience, for example, and it will be found that all this is due to the moon, to those beings who separated their substance from the earth with the moon. The presence of moon substances in the earth would have prevented the inner mobility of soul life.

We must remember that it was not merely for the sake of man that the separation of the sun and moon from the earth came to pass, but also for the sake of those beings whose evolution was at first bound to that of humanity. In the sun dwell beings who need the sun for their evolution, just as the evolution of man needs the earth. To remain with the earth would have been death to their existence; but the separation resulted in their becoming able by degrees to reach a stage where their beneficent influences could flow down to the earth from without. When the seer observes the light, when he perceives external objects, he realizes at a certain stage of his evolution that it is the sun beings which live behind the physical phenomena of colour, sound, and so on, but that these beings themselves had to develop to their present stage. These sun spirits are the upper spiritual beings contacted through the phenomena of the sense world.

Let us now ask how the inner stimulus was given to save mankind from hardening, from ossification. Certain beings were needed which at the appropriate time withdrew the moon substances from the earth. These beings realized that the act of the sun beings was not sufficient, and that they must protect the earth from ossification by withdrawing the moon from the earth. They were in a certain respect higher than the sun spirits. These latter, when the sun was still united with the earth, felt themselves obliged for the sake of their development to find another dwelling place, but the other spirits were able to remain with the earth even after the sun spirits had gone out. And this made it possible for them to save human evolution at a certain point of time by separating the moon from the earth. Thus they were in a certain respect higher than the sun beings—they were able to separate a substance from the earth relatively coarser than that connected with the sun spirits and by becoming rulers of this coarse substance to prove their greater power. For those who are able to transform evil into good are more powerful than those who rule over the good and make it, possibly, a little better.

Those are the beings behind the phenomena of the life of the soul who, by separating the moon from the earth, made thinking, feeling, willing and conscience possible. They come from the moon region, a spiritual kingdom which in a certain respect is higher, more powerful than that of the sun spirits, which are to be found behind external maya. Maya is twofold; there is the external maya of the sense world, and the inner maya of soul life. Behind the first stand those spiritual beings who have their centre in the sun; behind the maya of the inner life stand the other beings who belong to a more powerful kingdom. Just here we can see the truth of Greek mythology as portrayed in the story of Orestes. Orestes is told by the ruling gods that he has performed a good deed, but the Erinyes approach him, and they are felt to be older beings than those belonging to the kingdom of Zeus—goddesses who take vengeance even though the external goddesses of the sun kingdom (the kingdom of Zeus) had given their consent to the act. Man is here confronted by beings of an older spiritual race, who intervene as a corrective in what he undertakes under the guidance and leadership of the beings who withdrew from the earth with the sun. This remarkable example clearly shows how the conceptions of ancient peoples, expressed in their mythology, confirm what spiritual investigations of today teach in another way.

At this point I ask you to bear in mind the fact that at a certain point of time during the Earth evolution a spiritual being whom we name the Christ, a being previously united to the sun, descended from the sun and, at the time of the life of Jesus of Nazareth, united Himself to the earth. The Christ Being entered into the body of Jesus of Nazareth. This is an absolutely unique phenomenon and cannot be thought of in the same connection as other occurrences here mentioned. It has been said that after the separation of the sun, the earth would have hardened if the moon had not also been ejected; human beings would have mummified. This is perfectly true for a very large part of earth life, but not for the whole of it. In spite of the withdrawal of sun and moon, something in the earth would have fallen a prey to death if the Christ event had not come to pass. Though the withdrawal of the moon made an inner soul life possible, yet it was the Christ's descent from the sun which gave this inner life a new stimulus.

When a spiritual seer looks back to the time preceding the Christ event, a striking vision comes before him. The external form of the earth, confronting the physical senses as maya, vanishes and something comparable to the human form appears, but only a form, a figure. To spiritual vision the outer mayavic earth (and I say the earth deliberately) changed into the form of man with arms outstretched in the shape of a cross, a male-female form. This reminds us of the wonderful words of Plato, words that he drew from the mysteries, that the world soul is crucified on the cross of the world's body. This is exactly the image which presents itself to the eye of the spiritual seer: the Christ died on the cross, and thereupon the earth, which had been mere form and figure, became filled with life. The coming of the Christ principle into the earth had something in common with the withdrawal of the moon; life poured into what otherwise would have remained mere form. To understand ancient times aright is to realize that they all lead up to the Christ event. Just as people of today look back to the Christ as a being who at a certain point of time entered into human evolution, so pre-Christian initiates all pointed to the coming of the Christ as foreshown by events. Nothing could have been a surer herald of the Christ than the mighty phenomenon, visible under certain conditions to spiritual sight, of the disappearance of the physical form of the earth and the vision of the world soul crucified on the world's body. In dim Indian antiquity it was said by the sages that when their spiritual vision arose they saw, deep down under the mountains of the earth, near its central point, a cross, and upon it a male-female human being, having on its right side the symbol of the sun and upon its left side the symbol of the moon, and over the rest of the body the various land and sea formations of the earth. That was the clairvoyant vision which the sages of ancient India had of the form waiting until our earth could be brought to life by the Christ principle. And inasmuch as those ancient sages pointed to the most important prophecy of the Christ event, they were justified, when they looked still more deeply into existence, in saying: The Christ will come because that which points to Him is in existence.

Ancient wisdom at its highest level becomes prophetic; it looks towards that which will come to pass in the future. What the future holds is entirely the result of the present, and so present spiritual vision can receive intimations of a spiritual event that is to take place in the future. Indications of the Christ event were not given in any outwardly abstract way, but were revealed to spiritual sight by the phenomenon of the world soul crucified on the cross of the world's body, waiting to receive the life of the Christ when He should unite Himself with the earth. The wisdom of all epochs is a harmonious unity if considered in its fundamentals. Starting from this point let us look at the wisdom of different epochs in a light that will reveal it in its true aspect.

LECTURE 4

Evolutionary Stages: Saturn, Sun, Moon, Earth

26 August 1909

In view of what has been said we may ask whether all the spiritual beings in existence are to be found behind the phenomena of the sense world, or whether there are others having no expression or manifestation in the physical world. Supersensible consciousness knows that although it is true that a spiritual being or spiritual fact is to be found behind every external phenomenon, yet there do exist spiritual beings having no expression in the physical world. Experiences await the initiate other than those whose projections or shadow images are thrown into the physical sense world. There exist, moreover, spiritual beings and spiritual facts that have no expression in the inner life of the soul, in the phenomena of conscience, thought, feeling and sensation ... The spiritual world is seen by the higher consciousness to embrace much more than can be experienced in the physical world.

Those of my readers who have studied earlier lectures on these subjects, will realize that a host of spiritual beings, at different stages of evolution, have been involved in what has come to pass in the human, animal, vegetable and mineral kingdoms during the course of our Earth evolution. All such beings intervene in some way or other in the evolutionary texture of the earth and of the kingdoms belonging to it. Behind the phenomena surrounding us is a richly constituted spiritual world, just as there was during the periods of Old Saturn, Old Sun and Old Moon. We must not attempt to understand these spiritual kingdoms by inventing permanent names for these spiritual beings. The names used are not, for the most part, intended to designate individualities, but offices or spheres of duties. So if a particular name is used in connection with a being active during the Old Sun period it cannot be applied in the same sense to that being as regards its work or function in the Earth evolution; it has progressed by that time. It is necessary to speak of these matters with great accuracy and precision.

The Earth period was not only preceded by three embodiments of the Earth globe, but by three mighty spiritual kingdoms, essentially different from one another when examined by supersensible consciousness. Investigation of the Old Saturn, Old Sun and Old Moon periods reveals many things which cannot be compared with anything we can name on the earth, and of which one can only speak by analogy.

It will be remembered that I have spoken of the Old Saturn period as being essentially one of warmth, or of fire; on Old Sun this warmth condensed to air, on Old Moon the air condensed to water, and on Earth the earth element appeared for the first time. But the application of our concept of fire or warmth directly to the evolution of Old Saturn would result in an incorrect picture, for the fire of Saturn differed essentially from the fire of our Earth. There is only one phenomenon which can legitimately be compared to the Saturn fire, and that is the fire which permeates the blood as warmth. This vital warmth, or life principle, is more or less comparable to the substance of which Old Saturn was entirely composed, and the physical fire of today is a descendant, a later product of the Saturn fire; in its external form as perceived in space, it has appeared for the first time on the earth. The warmth of the blood, then, is the only thing which can be compared to what was present during the physical evolutionary period of Old Saturn. There is very little indeed in the realm of our present-day experience which can be compared in any way with the qualities of these earlier evolutionary periods, all of which were very different from our present earth existence.

It must be understood, however, that everything in the Saturn, Old Sun and Old Moon periods is comprised within the Earth evolution, only it has changed in character. What was laid as a germ on Old Saturn and evolved through the Old Sun and Old Moon periods is to be found in the Earth evolution, although in a changed condition. We can, however, instance the fundamental elements brought over from the earlier evolutionary periods by examining what is not to be found in this transformed state.

When the earth first appeared it had absorbed into itself three preceding evolutionary conditions, and all the degrees of spiritual beings involved in them. The beings were at different stages of evolution, however, so it is obvious that distinction must be made between these three different realms of spiritual beings and of spiritual substances; we must realize, in considering the beginnings of the earth, that certain things which we find there could come into existence only because the Old Saturn, Old Sun and Old Moon periods preceded our Earth evolution, and at its beginning the three are united within it.

This fact was always present in the ancient, instinctive consciousness of man, which connected him with the spiritual world. And when the number Three was mentioned as characteristic of the higher worlds, those individuals who looked at things in the concrete and not in the abstract, who had facts rather than conceptions or ideas in their mind's eye, always felt in their souls the truth that our earth has received into her womb as it were everything that came over from Old Saturn, Old Sun and Old Moon. That is the so-called higher, pre-terrestrial triad ... This triad consisting of Old Saturn, Old Sun and Old Moon has evolved into our earth. In its concrete meaning the higher triad signifies these three pre-terrestrial states; but the quaternary refers to the gradual transformation of these three into the earth. Accordingly men whose instinctive consciousness brought them into touch with the realities of the spiritual world felt the mystery of the birth of the earth to be expressed by the relation of three to four. And they turned reverent eyes to the sacred triad of Old Saturn, Old Sun and Old Moon, which had become the quaternary manifested by the Earth period. It is obvious that the modern expressions Saturn, Sun and Moon had other equivalents in the instinctive consciousness of ancient humanity.

If we now follow up the course of the Earth evolution we may ask how the separate classes of spiritual beings participate in its progress. Spiritual beings at different stages of evolution directed the processes of the separation of the sun and moon from the earth, as a result of which that progress came to pass. We have first to consider a class of spiritual beings which attained a certain stage of evolution during the Old Sun period; they belong to the Old Sun evolution because it was destined to provide a field of action for them. These are beings which during the current Earth period separated the sun from the earth, because during Old Sun they had been Sun-bound in the same way as humanity is now earthbound. As we have seen, during the current Earth period they needed the sun for their further evolution and with the sun they left the earth in order to work upon the latter from without. When these spirits had withdrawn, the Old Saturn and Old Moon spirits, who had gone through on Old Saturn and Old Moon respectively the stage that humanity is now going through, were still left on the earth. However, the development of the Old Saturn spirits was such that they were now able to direct and guide the separation of the moon from the earth. They had passed through the same stage on Old Saturn as the spirits who had already removed the sun from the earth had done on Old Sun; they were more mature than the spirits who had separated with the sun, and they were therefore able to separate the moon from the earth and to stimulate the inner development of man from within—otherwise man would have hardened and become mummified. It may be said that the withdrawal of the sun was brought about by the Old Sun spirits, and that of the moon by the Old Saturn spirits. The sun has thus become a cosmic symbol for the act of the Old Sun spirits, the moon for that of the Old Saturn spirits; and the spirits who during the Old Moon period went through the stage that humanity is now going through were left upon the earth itself.

It will be useful at this point to bear in mind a definite epoch of the Earth evolution, that at which the moon had just left the earth. The earth, from which the sun had withdrawn still earlier, was then in a very different condition from that of today. If the earth had then been in an exactly similar state to that of today, the whole process would have been unnecessary.

It was, compared to the present mineral, vegetable, animal and human kingdoms, very imperfect in that early period. The various continents had not separated off from each other; everything was in a kind of chaos. Supersensible sight would search in vain at that period for the mineral, vegetable, animal and human kingdoms as they are today. These forms have all developed as a result of the influence of the sun and the moon from without, and this was the purpose of the withdrawal of these two bodies. The influences which worked upon the earth from the sun and the moon charmed from it, as it were, everything that has since arisen upon it and all that surrounds us today. The outer forms of the minerals, the plants, the animals and of physical man have been produced by the beings which work from the sun; whereas the beings which work from the moon have stimulated the soul life of human beings and of animals. This is an approximate and broad sketch of evolution from the so-called Lemurian epoch on into that of Atlantis. It was during the Atlantean epoch that, very slowly and gradually, the earth began to wear an appearance more or less similar to that which we see around us today. It is necessary, therefore, in the course of its evolution since the withdrawal of the moon, to distinguish between a chaotic earth and an organized earth that has been influenced by the spiritual beings in its environment.

What is here stated need not necessarily be acquired from historical tradition. Suppose for example that the initiate wisdom of ancient and venerable India, of the Persian sages, of the Egyptian initiations, or of the Greek mysteries had all been lost; suppose no external documents of any kind whatever were left to tell us of the pristine teaching concerning the spiritual foundations of our Earth evolution. Even then the possibility of developing supersensible consciousness would not be lost; everything that is said here can be discovered by means of supersensible investigation without the aid of any historical document. We have to do with something which at the present time can be studied at its source; even mathematics may also be learnt from original sources.

Let us now try to find a link between the results which supersensible investigation has given us and life in ancient times. It is obvious that some other method might be adopted, but the purpose of this course of lectures is to compare what can be found irrespective of any historical record with what has been handed down by another kind of tradition. We will go back, not so very far, to a historical personage who lived in a comparatively ancient period of Greek culture, of whom history knows very little and the length of whose life even is veiled in much uncertainty. Pherecydes of Syros is in a certain respect the forerunner of the other Greek sages. He lived at a time in Greek spiritual development called the epoch of the Seven Sages. This period preceded that of all historical Greek philosophy.

The little that external history tells us of Pherecydes of Syros is very interesting. He, among others, is spoken of as the teacher of Pythagoras; and many of the teachings of Herakleitos, of Plato and of later sages can be traced back to him. It is said that he taught the existence of three principles fundamental to the whole of evolution, and called them Zeus, Kronos and Chthon. Now what precisely did he mean by these names? It will at once be realized that Kronos is only another name for the Old Saturn evolution. In the teaching of Pherecydes, Kronos is the totality of spiritual beings belonging to the kingdom of Old Saturn, who during the course of Earth evolution were able to bring about the separation of the moon. Now for Zeus! Zeus is a word of uncertain meaning when used in ancient times, for it was applied to spiritual individualities at very different stages of evolution. But people in ancient Greece who know something of initiation recognized in Zeus the ruler of the sun spirits. Zeus lives in the influences which came to the earth from the sun. Chthon is a designation of the somewhat chaotic condition of the earth after the withdrawal of the moon, at which time no plant or animal or human forms were to be found. In most remarkable words, Pherecydes spoke of the holy primordial triad, of Zeus, Kronos and Chthon, principles fundamental to the earth, having come over from pre-terrestrial ages; he also speaks of a further evolution. But in ancient times people did not clothe matters of this kind in such dry, crude concepts as they do today; they drew vivid pictures of what they saw and recognized in spiritual realms. Pherecydes said: 'Chthon becomes Gaia (today called earth), because of the gift of Zeus whereby she came to be covered as with a garment.' This is a wonderful description of that evolution which I have just outlined in a few short words. The earth was alone; outside it were the sun and the moon, the spiritual kingdoms of Zeus and of Kronos. The sun from without began to work upon the earth and to fructify it in its then chaotic state. Or, in the language of the old Greek sage, Zeus fructified Chthon. The beneficent influences of the kingdom of Zeus were sent down to the physical earth in the warmth and light of the sun. This was the gift made by Zeus to the earth. The earth covered herself with the garment of plant and animal forms, and with the forms of physical human beings. Chthon becomes Gaia; therefore, because of the gift of Zeus the earth covers herself with a garment.

This is a wonderful picture, expressed in beautiful language, of what supersensible consciousness is able today to rediscover in the epoch of the Seven Greek Sages. And Pherecydes could not have made such strikingly vivid statements, which can be verified by modern supersensible consciousness, without definite personal knowledge. This knowledge he derived from the so-called Phoenician initiation. He was an initiate of the temples of ancient Phoenicia and had brought over into Greece the temple wisdom which he was at liberty to teach. A great deal of oriental wisdom came over in this way.

This is one example, among many, of the things that may be rediscovered in the words of the old sages independently of historical tradition. In this instance we have not gone back so very far in human history. If we are able rightly to interpret the expressions used, it is also possible to rediscover original teachings of very ancient times. It would, however, be false to accept the simple explanation that this or that eastern teaching concerning the evolution of the world is found under the same form in Pherecydes of Syros, in the old Egyptian epoch, in the days of the Chaldean sages, and in the ancient Indian period. If this were the case, it might well be imagined that a wisdom rediscovered today is to be found, in different form, wherever humanity has striven after it; that wisdom is one and the same at all times and in all places. In its abstract sense there is not the slightest objection to be raised to this statement; it is true, but it expresses only a portion of the whole truth. Just as from the rest of a plant to the fruit there is not a regular succession of similar forms, but a variety, composed of green leaves, coloured petals, stamens, etc., of higher and higher development, so does diversity appear in the progress of human life on earth. Correct though it is to say that the same wisdom appears again and again in different forms, an evolution or a development does nevertheless take place; and it is not at all correct to say that we find in ancient Indian times exactly the same conditions as exist today. That would be as inaccurate as to state that the blossom of a plant is the same as the root. True, the same force exists within it, but the reality emerges only if progress and development are recognized to be fundamental expressions of the secrets underlying human evolution. The teachings of the first post-Atlantean epoch may still be given today; what Pherecydes of Syros taught can be repeated today. But the Earth evolution has also been enriched, and impulses have since been poured into it.

The importance of the Christ impulse in human evolution has already been indicated. That is a thing apart, standing alone in the evolution of the earth; there is nothing which can be compared with it. It has come to my knowledge that people have spoken of injustice in connection with human evolution if it were true that for so many thousands of years before the coming of the Christ full wisdom could not be imparted to mankind. Why was it, these people ask, that anything could be withheld from pre-Christian men. They seem to think, in view of the fact that justice is universal, that although the forms of truth have changed new truths cannot have been added to the old; for if it were otherwise, people living in the Christian era would be destined to receive something higher than those of pre-Christian times. Now it is understandable that such things should be said in the outer world, but it is not understandable that students of spiritual science should make such statements. And why? Because the people who incarnate during the Christian era are those who have passed through previous incarnations, and what they could not possibly learn before the appearance of Christ on earth they must learn after that event. Anyone who believes that man incarnates again and again only to learn exactly the same wisdom has no serious appreciation and feeling for reincarnation in his soul; for to believe in reincarnation seriously means to realize its goal and its purpose and to know that there is good reason for our returning to earth repeatedly. We come back in order to have new experiences. It is a platitude to say that exactly the same wisdom is to be met with again and again in different conceptions of the world. The concrete fact is that wisdom develops, that it takes on higher and higher forms, until there comes into being on the earth something that is ripe to pass over into another condition, in the same way as Old Saturn, Old Sun and Old Moon passed over to the earth condition. There is real progress and not mere repetition—that is the whole point. And here lies the difference between eastern and western modes of thought. Western thought, in face of the whole task and mission of the West, can never separate itself from an actual, a concrete historical conception of the evolution of the Earth; and a historical conception implies the idea of progress, not of mere repetition.

It was in the West that the real concept of historical development arose. If anyone falls into a purely oriental way of thought (and its truth is not in any way questioned, only the historical sense must be added to it) because he has not grasped the idea of historical progress, he may easily lose sight of the meaning of history altogether. He may find himself faced with the question: What is the purpose of this eternal repetition or recurrence of the same thing? That was a problem raised by Schopenhauer who had no understanding of history in its real sense, and whose exoteric teaching was influenced in high degrees by what he had absorbed from oriental life. Statement of a higher truth in no way impugns a lower, lesser truth; spiritual science fully assents to statements of a non-historical nature in oriental spiritual life. But the point at issue here is that of raising a mode of thinking to a higher level or, as we may say, of illuminating oriental thought by the light of the West.

What I have said here in general terms I should like to illustrate by an example. From what has been said it will be realized that the discoveries of modern supersensible investigation are to be found under another form in ancient times, if we look for them there. It is only possible to throw light on antiquity by starting from the present. Let us in this connection take a definite spiritual individuality. If we go back to a time when men brought down into the Vedas what was in a certain respect an echo of the sublime wisdom of the Holy Rishis, we find, among many appellations of divine beings, the name of Indra. If, from the point of view of modern supersensible investigation, I were to give an answer to the question, 'What kind of being is the Indra mentioned in the Vedas?' it would be best for me to explain how it is possible for a modern person to acquire a conception of that being by means of spiritual sight. We have already seen that by rising from the physical to the soul world spiritual beings can be perceived behind everything surrounding us in the world—behind fire, air, water and earth, which are their external expressions or manifestations. In the spiritual realm behind the element of air, for instance, a host of spiritual beings appear, beings which do not descend so far as the physical world but express themselves therein through the air. In the soul world we meet them as entities, as individualities, and the mightiest of them is still to be found today in him who in ancient India was named 'Indra'. Indra is associated with the whole regulation of man's breathing process, and to his activity we owe the fact that we breathe as we do today. Humanity may look up to this being forever and realize that it is the mighty Indra who has endowed them with the instrument of breath. The activities of such a being are not however limited to one sphere, and humanity owes much else to Indra; they owe to Indra the force which must pour through their muscles if their enemies are to be conquered in war. Hence people were able to pray to mighty Indra for power to be victorious in battle, since this also was one of his functions. To this same being (which needs no name if only its presence is realized) is to be ascribed the flashing of the lightning effects of storms. For these things, too, prayers may be raised, if, in the praying, the gods are thought of.

Indra exists for us today as he existed in ancient Vedic times, but we must now pass on to another consideration. Suppose we take this being named Indra as actually seen by the old Indian initiates when their spiritual sight was opened in the soul world, and ask ourselves whether the initiate of modern days sees him in the same form. The answer is that he does, in fact, see everything perceptible to the ancient initiate, but something else as well. To take a rather trivial example, suppose we consider a man in the fortieth year of his life and call him Muller. He is the same person who 30 years previously was a boy of ten, but he has changed, even if his name is the same. It would be incorrect to describe this man Muller as a man of 40 using his appearance at the age of ten; he has passed through a certain development, which must be taken into account when speaking of him in his present condition. Is it to be imagined, then, that while men on the earth continually develop during their single lives and also from life to life, spiritual beings remain at the same stage at which they manifested themselves to the spiritual consciousness of an ancient Indian initiate? Is it right to conceive of the gods as remaining unchanged through thousands of years? It certainly is not. Indra has passed through an evolution since the days when seers of ancient India looked up to him with reverence. Now what has happened to this mighty figure of Indra, and how does his evolution manifest itself if we look back upon it with spiritual consciousness? At a certain moment in evolution something very remarkable with regard to Indra comes to pass. In order to have a clear conception we must repeat certain things. We will direct our spiritual consciousness in the soul world to the ancient Indian god Indra and follow him through thousands of years. We come to a point of time when there is an appearance of rays of light falling from an entirely different spiritual being upon Indra, who is illumined by them and ascends to a higher stage of development. It is rather like learning something important from another individual at a certain age, which changed one's whole life. This happened in the case of great Indra, and since that time there has streamed from him the same influence as was to be found in ancient India, only enriched by the spiritual light of another being which was shed upon him. It is possible to indicate the precise moment in the history of the evolution of humanity when this took place. The god Indra is to be found in the soul world at a time when the Christ was not yet perceptible to Earth evolution, although the Christ light shone upon him. A man who is able to perceive Indra may well say that this being now reveals something different from his earliest revelations; for at first the Christ light did not ray back from him. Since the point of time in question, Indra has not shed his own light into the spiritual evolution of the earth, but has reflected the light of Christ, just as the moon reflects the light of the sun.

The light thus rayed back by Indra, not directly perceptible on earth and in which therefore we cannot actually recognize Christ, was proclaimed by Moses to his people. Moses gave the name of Yahweh or Jehovah to this Christ light rayed back by Indra as the sunlight is reflected by the moon. In lectures on the Gospel of St John, I have spoken about another aspect of this matter. The Christ is heralded, and Yahweh or Jehovah is the name of the Christ light rayed back by an ancient deity. It is a prophetic heralding of Christ. Indra himself passed to a higher stage of evolution through this contact with the Christ light. He did not of course become Jehovah. It is not correct to say that Jehovah is Indra. But we can understand that as Indra manifests himself in lightning and thunder even so does Jehovah manifest Himself therein, because a being can only reflect in accordance with its own nature. Jehovah therefore was manifested in lightning and thunder.

This is an instance of spiritual being accomplished in its own realm in the same way as human evolution in our world, and of the fact that the same picture of the spiritual beings is not forthcoming after the lapse of thousands of years. History is being made in the spiritual world, and earth history is only the outer expression of this spiritual history. Every earthly occurrence has its course in events of the spiritual world, and it is necessary to understand these spiritual events in detail.

By this example I have tried to show what it means to throw light upon antiquity from a modern point of view. History is a concept which must be taken quite seriously, and the instance given should elucidate spiritual life. If we bear in mind the fact that there are wisdom-beings to be found today by occult research which we encounter again when we go back in time, only under different names and different manifestations—and at the same time remember that his-torical evolution and progress are realities in spiritual life—which underlie all that is physical, we have grasped two principles of fundamental importance to all progressive spiritual science that is to influence the future of humanity.

LECTURE 5

The Children of Lucifer and the Brothers of Christ

27 August 1909

In the preceding lecture it has been shown to what extent the external world is an illusion, concealing the spiritual world behind it. The consciousness of the seer penetrating through this illusion represents one path to the spiritual world. It has, however, also been shown that everything in the inner life of the soul, thinking, feeling, sensations, as also the more complicated phenomena of conscience, and so on, form a kind of veil concealing a spiritual world. And the consciousness of the seer penetrating these veils represents the other path into the spiritual world. The existence of these two different paths has been known at all times to people who sought for initiation. Hence we find that a distinction was made by ancient peoples between upper and lower gods. In the mysteries of all epochs it was taught that at a certain stage of initiation man enters the world of the upper and of the lower gods, but a great distinction was made between them. Man has no influence upon the way in which the outer world confronts him in the many coloured tapestry of colour impressions, warmth impressions, etc., or in the phenomena of the elements of fire, air, water and earth. The sun rises in the morning; it sheds its rays of light over the earth, and according to the different conditions set up, the external world of the senses appears. When man penetrates through these outer phenomena, he reaches the spiritual world.

Man is not in a position to destroy this world of the senses through his own resources, because he cannot materially affect the outer phenomena surrounding him. The sense world is placed before him by the spiritual beings of whom it is an expression and manifestation; through his own power he cannot impair it. At initiation he is able to penetrate the veil of the sense world, but he must leave it just as the spiritual beings have shaped and fashioned it.

The relation of a human being to his own inner life is different. His perceptions, feelings, will, his thinking and the development of his conscience depend upon the extent to which he has worked upon the evolution of his soul life. Man cannot evoke a pure or an impure red or green colour from the dawn or from a plant. But the corruption of his soul life may well give rise to grotesque feelings and bad moral judgements. He can submit in a greater or lesser degree to the dictation of his conscience; in his fancies he can devote himself to beauty or to ugliness, to true or to false thought images. Through his own conduct a man modifies or changes the veil spread over the spiritual world by the inner life of the soul. And because what we see behind the veil of our own soul life depends upon whether this veil itself is pure or corrupt, it is easy to understand that in cases where the inner life is corrupt or but slightly developed then when the ascent into the spiritual worlds or descent to the realm of lower spiritual beings takes place grotesque images in the form of false, nonsensical abnormal concepts and forces may be called into being. As a result it came about that in every age a distinction was made between the ascent to the upper gods and the descent to the lower gods, and the descent to the lower gods was regarded as more essentially dangerous than the ascent to the upper gods; and on this latter path through the veils of the inner life to the spiritual worlds, very high demands were made of the pupil of the mysteries and of occult science.

Mention had to be made of this, because these two paths to the spiritual world have played a great role in human evolution, and the East and the West, and the relation between the 'Children of Lucifer' and the 'Brothers of Christ' can only be rightly understood if their existence is taken into account. In the outer world, which to the ordinary human eye is apt to appear a motley web of many and varied facts and phenomena, there is nothing which is not guided by wisdom, nothing in which spiritual beings, spiritual forces and facts do not come into play; and we understand the matter aright only when we have realized that the spiritual events have been brought together under the direction of those powers which have been described from many different aspects. To understand why a certain form of wisdom has flourished in the East and why the future of the Christian impulse depends upon the development of powers residing in the West, we must consider the origin and historical trend of the two worlds (East and West).

We know that the spiritual life of the present had its origin in old Atlantis, that an ancient spiritual life developed upon a land in the west lying between modern Europe and America, and that such Asiatic, African and American civilizations as exist are the last remnants of those of ancient Atlantis. Atlantis is the Father and Motherland of all the cultured life of today. Before the mighty catastrophe which changed the face of the globe into its present configuration, there were to be found in old Atlantis species of human beings very different from those of the present time, who were guided by high initiates and leaders. A civilization developed there essentially under the influence of an ancient clairvoyance, and people possessed a natural and instinctive faculty for penetrating through the outer veils of the sense world to the higher spiritual world as well as through their own soul life to the lower gods. Just as it is natural to people of the present day to see with their eyes, hear with their ears, and so on, it was natural for people of that time not only to see colours and hear in the outer world but to be aware of spiritual beings as realities behind these colours and tones. In the same way it was natural for people at that time not only to hear the voice of conscience but also to perceive those spiritual beings called Erinyes by the Greeks. The old Atlanteans were intimately acquainted with a spiritual world. The purpose of human evolution implies that people are gradually to rise up out of this old instinctive but spiritually perceptive consciousness and push forward to the consciousness proper to our modern time. It was necessary for people to go through this stage of life on the physical plane. It was not possible to guide the whole evolution of mankind from the spiritual world in such a simple way that one stream of humanity should pass from old Atlantis over the regions of Europe and Africa into Asia, and that everything should develop, as it were, along straight lines. Evolution is never a simple, straight line of development from a single germ; another factor has to come in, and a very simple analogy will show that this is the case. Consider a plant. The seed is put into the earth and out of it develop the elementary organs of the plant, the leaves and, later, the calyx, stamen, pistils and so on. Now if development is to continue in plant life, as we know it, it is essential that something else should happen. The formation of the fruit from the blossom depends upon fecundation; the fertilizing substances of one plant must pass over to another, for the fruit could not develop simply out of the blossom. A stream of influences from outside has to be introduced in order that development may progress. What may be perceived in the plant is a picture of universal life and is also an indication of the laws of spiritual life. It is quite false to believe that in spiritual life a stream of culture arises here or there and continually produces new offshoots from itself. This may happen for a time, but it would no more suffice to bring about what is to come to pass than would the blossom, without fertilization, be able to produce the fruit. At a certain definite point of cultural evolution, a side influence must come in, a spiritual fertilization of human development. Just

as in plant life the male and female elements develop independently, so in human evolution from the time of Atlantis
there had to be formed not one stream but two, passing from
old Atlantis towards the East. It was necessary that these
streams of civilization should develop separately for a while,
and then meet again to fertilize each other at a definite
period.

We can follow these two streams of human evolution if we
examine the records of spiritual seership. One stream of
evolution is formed by the transmigration of certain peoples
from old Atlantis to more northerly regions, touching terri-
tories which now include England, the north of France, and
thence extend to the present Scandinavia, Russia and into
Asia as far as India. In this movement were to be found
peoples of various kinds, forming the vehicle of a definite
spiritual life. A second stream went a different way, in a more
southerly direction, through southern Spain and Africa to
Egypt and thence to Arabia. Each of these two streams of
civilization goes its own way until they meet to fructify each
other at a later point of time.

Now wherein consists the difference between these two
streams of culture? People belonging to the northern stream
were more adapted for the use of the outer senses of external
perception; their tendency was to look outwards to the veil of
the surrounding world. There were initiates among these
northern people who showed them the way to the spiritual
worlds where the upper gods were to be found—gods who
are reached by penetrating through the veils of the outer
sense world. To this category belong the beings reverenced
as the northern Germanic gods. Odin, Thor, etc. are the
names of divine beings to be found behind the outer veil of
the sense world. People belonging to the southern stream
were differently constituted. These peoples had a greater
tendency to delve into their soul life, into their inner nature.
Let us say—and do not take the word amiss—the northern

peoples had a greater gift for observing the world, the southern peoples for brooding over their own soul life, seeking the spiritual world through this inner veil. Hence it is not a matter for wonder that the gods of the descendants of the southern stream belonged to the Nether World and were rulers of the soul life. Consider the Egyptian Osiris. Osiris is the divinity found by man on passing through the gate of death; Osiris is the god who cannot live in the external sense world. He lived there in ancient times only, and as the new era approached he was overcome by the powers of the sense world, by the evil Set; and since then he has lived in the world entered after death, accessible only by plunging into the immortal, permanent human principle which passes from incarnation to incarnation. This was why Osiris was felt to be most intimately bound up with the inner life of man.

Here we have the fundamental difference between the northern and the southern peoples. There was, however, one race who in the first period of the post-Atlantean epoch combined both qualities. This race was specially selected to follow both paths leading to the spiritual world and along each of them to discover that which was serviceable and right for that epoch, being possessed of the capacity both for attaining the spiritual world behind the external sense world and also for finding the spiritual world behind the veil of their own soul life by sinking into the mystical depths of their inner nature.

This faculty, in the first epochs at all events of the old Atlantean era, was possessed by all people—and connected with it was a very definite experience. If a person who is only able to reach the spiritual world through the external sense world and to find the upper gods hears that somewhere else on the earth there are other gods, he does not understand them aright. But where the two faculties of penetrating through the external sense world and through the veil of the soul life are united, a person makes the very significant discovery that what is to be found behind the veil of the soul life is exactly the same, in essence, as that behind the veil of the outer sense world. A uniform spiritual world is revealed from without and from within. If a person should get to know the spiritual world by both paths, he realizes their unity. The people of ancient India were in a position to realize the unity of spiritual life. When the supersensible sight of the ancient Indian was directed outwards he perceived spiritual beings holding together and coordinating external phenomena. When he sank into his inner nature he found his Brahman; and he knew what he found behind the veil of his soul life to be identical with that which, passing through the cosmos on mighty pinions, created and fashioned the external world. Such mighty conceptions—fruits of ancient Atlantean culture, preserved over the post-Atlantean times—still influence us.

But evolution, remember, does not progress by the mere transformation or preservation of the old, but by the bringing to birth of other streams of evolution so that mutual enrichment may take place. If we follow up the northern stream of evolution into Asia, we find that the Indian people travelled the farthest, and after amalgamation with other elements, built up ancient Indian culture. But more to the north, in the region of Persia, we find an ancient civilization known in later history as the Zarathustrian culture. When we investigate this Zarathustrian culture with supersensible sight we find that the characteristic of its people was to look more to the outer world, and to advance towards the spiritual world by this path. In view of this characteristic it is evident why Zarathustra, the leader of this ancient Persian culture, attached less importance to inner, mystical absorption, and why he was in a way opposed to it. Zarathustra pointed more particularly to the external sense world and to the visible sun, in order to call people's attention to the existence behind this visible sun of a spiritual solar being, Ahura Mazda. This is an exact instance of the path followed by initiates of the northern peoples. The highest form of this more external realization of the spiritual world was developed in ancient Persian culture under the leadership of the original Zarathustra. This form of outer perception was less and less perfect for peoples the further they had lagged behind the ancient Persians who had pressed on to western Asia. Other peoples remained behind in Asia and Europe, but the tendency of them all was to look more towards the external world, and all their initiates chose the path of pointing out to their followers the spiritual world behind the veil of the outer sense world. If we make use of spiritual sight, we find in Europe, in that wonderful Celtic culture which really underlies all other European culture, the remnant of what arose as a result of the cooperation of the mind of the peoples with the wisdom of the initiates. Today Celtic wisdom has very largely been lost, and can be deciphered only to a certain extent by those who have spiritual vision. Wherever ancient Celticism still shines out as the fundamental basis of other European civilizations, there you have an echo of still older European civilizations which, although their paths were in reality the same, remained with the mighty Zarathustrian culture in so far as the characteristics of their peoples were concerned. According to the external distribution of the people their path to the spirit differed.

It must be understood that the interplay of man with the external world, whether it be the external spiritual world or the external sense world, has no effect upon him. Experiences that arise are not a kind of cosmic reflection, but exist in order to bring about the progress of humanity in a perfectly definite way. Now, in reality what is man of a particular epoch? Man is the result or product of the activities of cosmic powers surrounding him, and is fashioned according to the way in which these cosmic powers permeate him. A person who inhales healthy air develops his organs correspondingly, and the same thing happens to the spiritual organism of a person who absorbs one or another kind of spiritual life and culture. Since the bodily organism is a product of the spiritual it is affected accordingly. Human evolution is a continuous process and so it is clear that in all the peoples of this northern stream the development of the external bodily qualities is noticeable, for the forces and powers of the outer world—everything that can fashion from without—were the special ones which streamed into them. Through these outer forces was developed what can be seen and perceived outwardly. Hence in these peoples, we find not only a development of warlike qualities but also an instrument of ever-increasing suitability for penetrating the external world: the brain itself grows to greater perfection under the influence of these external forces. The fundamental factors, therefore, for understanding the external world are present in people belonging to this northern stream, and only from them could be derived that spiritual culture which led finally to the mastery of the powers and forces of external nature. It may be said that the principal task of these people consisted in perfecting man's outer instrument, that part of him which is perceptible from without, not only in a physical but also in an intellectual, moral and aesthetic sense. More and more of the spirit was poured into the outer corporeality. Physical corporeality was developed to greater and greater perfection, and so the individual souls passing from one incarnation to another were generally able to find better vehicles in succeeding births, not only in a physical but also in a moral sense.

Now let us enquire what special characteristic developed among the peoples who took the more southern way. It was of course the refinement of the life of the soul, the inner life. The conception of conscience is not to be found in olden times among those peoples whose task was the spiritualization of the outer corporeal qualities. Conscience as a conception arises from among the southern peoples; among them the inner life of the soul was enriched with ideas and conceptions to such an extent that it finally developed into that wealth of secret hermetic science possessed by the ancient Egyptians which amazes us even today. The wisdom of the Egyptians, held in such high honour by those who have knowledge of such matters, could only arise as the result of the development of the inner soul life. All the art and the wisdom which man had to develop from within appeared in the stream of evolution, wherein less importance was attached to the spiritualization of the external corporeality than to the refinement and elaboration of the inner forces of the soul.

Let us now consider Greek sculpture. When a Greek sculptor wished to represent a physical body purified and spiritualized, he produced a type of the northern peoples. All the external forms of Zeus, of Aphrodite, of Pallas Athene, are racial types of the north. Where it was a matter of indicating the inner development of the life of the soul, it was necessary to show that forces develop invisibly within the soul, and then such a figure as Hermes or Mercury was produced. The form of Hermes is that of the African peoples, and it differs from the figures of the other gods; the ears are different, so is the hair, and the eyes are narrow and unlike the eyes of the northern types. It was known that this type of humanity represented the vehicle of the scientific element, of wisdom, of everything which works upon the soul, and with this was connected the conception of Hermes as messenger to the lower gods.

Again we might characterize the difference between the two evolutionary streams by saying that the northern peoples worked at the production of a human being whose outer bodily form is an image of the spirit; whereas the southern peoples were busy developing the invisible forces of soul, perceptible only when the gaze is directed inwards (to the inner life). The northern races created the outer aspect of the image of divinity in man; the southern peoples created the invisible soul-image of the Godhead in the inner life.

Thus the gods of the southern peoples are invisible divinities which man contacts in his inner nature, who arouse a certain fear and dread, but who from another aspect inspire trust and confidence. It has been pointed out that a man sees these gods of the inner world according to his own nature. If he is morally developed he confronts these gods with moral qualities of soul and their true image is revealed; their essence flows into him and he experiences inner illumination and enlightenment. If a man is immoral and his conceptions are bad, or ugly, or untrue he perceives a distorted image of this world of the gods; fearful demoniacal shapes and figures appear, even as the most beautiful face is twisted and caricatured if observed in a spherical mirror. This is why a man confronting these inner gods might feel them to be friendly, intimate spiritual companions, pouring forces into the very depths of soul life, belonging to him in the most intimate sense, strengthening and illuminating him. But if he saw them in images distorted by his own qualities, horror and terror might arise; he could be tormented, persecuted and led to the wildest excesses of life just because of their manifestation in the grotesque image of his lower passions. From this we may judge why care was taken that no unprepared human being should meet these particular gods. But where access was made possible to the spiritual world a preliminary development of the moral nature was imperatively demanded, and a very thorough preparation was ensured. The initiates were never tired of giving warning about the dangers awaiting weak souls at the meeting with these gods.

In accordance with the nature of the powers holding sway in the spiritual world accessible to the southern peoples it is called the world of Lucifer, the Light-bearer. It is a world, spiritual and divine in its nature, illumined in the inner being of man by a light invisible to outward sight and which has to be acquired by the process of individual perfecting. This was the path to the world of Lucifer which people of the southern evolutionary stream took.

As we have seen, the ideal before the more northern stream was the production of a human individuality so perfect, so full of spirit, so noble in regard to everything in life between birth and death that the outer body should be a worthy vessel for spirituality of the very highest order. And in Zarathustra, the being who had most truly shown the way to the spiritual world behind the veil of sense phenomena, there arose the thought that an outer body must be created by so moral, intellectual and spiritual a force as should bring it to the highest point of spirituality of which an external body is capable. And since this thought first arose in Zarathustra, he set himself the task of reaching an increasingly lofty standard of perfection, living through every succeeding incarnation in bodies of higher moral, aesthetic and intellectual qualities. Zarathustra, then, brought these physical qualities to such a point of excellence that his body became not a mere image of the divine world of spirit, but a vessel for the reception of the Godhead otherwise to be seen only behind the veil of the sense world. That to which the old Zarathustra had pointed as the world of sun beings behind the physical sun, as the hidden spirit of the Good—Ahura Mazda—needed, as it approached nearer and nearer to the earth, to find a dwelling place within a body of great spiritual perfection. And so in one of his incarnations, Zarathustra appeared in the body of Jesus of Nazareth, a body so spiritualized, so noble that into its external corporeality could be poured that spiritual essence formerly to be found only behind the veil of the sense world. The human body which had been developed in the northern evolutionary stream by the turning of the external gaze to the spiritual world was prepared for the reception of the spiritual essence concealed behind the sense world. For in this manner, preparation was made for the mighty event of the reception upon earth of the spirit behind the sense world, invisible to all save spiritual sight, and its maturing there for three years in the body of Jesus of Nazareth. Hence it devolved upon the northern peoples not only to develop an understanding of what lay behind the sense world, but to prepare for the possibility of that spirit flooding our earthly world, of the being heretofore hidden behind the sun, treading the earth for three years, as man among men.

Thus Lucifer had entered into humanity in the southern peoples, and Christ into the northern peoples, each in conformity with the characteristics of the two streams of evolution. We ourselves live at a time when the two streams must unite as the male and female fertilizing substances of plants coalesce; we live at a time when the Christ who was drawn from outside as an objective being into the purified body of Jesus of Nazareth must be understood through deep contemplation on the part of the soul, and its union with the world of spirit to be discovered in the inner being, the world arising from Lucifer's kingdom. In this way will come to pass the mutual fertilization of these two evolutionary streams of humanity. It has already begun; it began at the moment indicated in the story which tells us that the sacrificial blood of the Christ flowing from the cross was received into the vessel of the Holy Grail and brought to the West from the East, where preparation for the understanding of the incarnation of Christ had been made in a very definite way by cultivating that which represents the light of Lucifer. In this way the union of these two streams in humanity will become more and more complete. Whatever mankind of the present time may say or do, the healing of the future humanity will be accomplished by the fact that within the union of the two streams the mighty Christ Being, guiding as He does the evolution of the universe and of man, is understood through the light received by the soul from within, out of the kingdom of Lucifer. Christ will give the substance, Lucifer the form, and from their union will arise impulses which shall permeate the spiritual evolution of mankind, and bring about what the future has in store for the healing and the blessing of the peoples.

LECTURE 6

Lucifer and Christ

28 August 1909

We have spoken of two spiritual streams, flowing through different peoples, and passing from old Atlantis towards the East. We saw the difference in their development and how they were enabled to prepare future events; and we observed how the southern stream more particularly tended to deepen the power of penetration to the spiritual world which lies behind the soul world of man, while the other more northerly spiritual stream directed man's attention to his earthly environment in order to make him aware of the spiritual world behind the world of the senses. Mention has been made of the development in the southern stream of qualities which led to spiritual beings connected with the luciferic principle, and of the gradual approach to earth, on the other side, of the kingly spiritual being behind the sun in order finally to incarnate in a physical body, which, through many incarnations of a certain individuality, had been so purified that the Godhead found in it not merely an image of itself but was able actually to incarnate within it. The incarnation of the Christ, the Sun Spirit, in the body of Jesus of Nazareth was the great event which took place in the northern stream of peoples. Now these two streams of peoples may be said to have moved towards each other in order to be mutually enriched, and during their progress there arose, in the first epoch after the great Atlantean catastrophe, the ancient Indian race in the south of Asia, a race in which the human soul was in a certain sense able to look out towards the external world of the senses as well as into itself to find the spirit, because it instinctively recognized the unity between the spirit in the external world and the spirit within man. Let us picture to ourselves the feelings of the ancient Indian when he looked out at the sense world, at the earth with its mountains and forests, its tapestry of plant life, its animal and human kingdoms.

Possessed in high degree of spiritual sight, this ancient Indian soul perceived, underlying everything, a spiritual world consisting of beings of etheric substance, who did not descend to the density of a physical body. In the mountains, trees and stars the soul of the ancient Indian saw not only the dense elements but also the finer, etheric nature, in the shape of the external world of the gods. It should not of course be imagined that these spirits were composed merely of ether. But just as the etheric, the astral and the 'I' principles are within the physical body of a man, so these spirits had an etheric body for their lowest principle and their other, higher principles in higher worlds. The Indian, looking into this world, felt that he stood upon the earth; that as man he had through long periods of time developed from the first germ of human existence on ancient Saturn down to the Earth evolution; that it was necessary for him to descend to dense physical matter in order to acquire self-consciousness within it. He said: 'I, speaking to myself, am an "I" being; formerly I was a companion of all those spiritual beings visible around me to spiritual sight from the etheric world upwards. I have descended from these worlds to denser matter, yet in them all human perfections are to be found, not only those now possessed by man but those which he will have to attain through his own efforts. But there is one thing which no being who does not descend to the physical plane can attain. There are in the universe other lofty perfections as well as the recollection peculiar to human consciousness. There are other kinds of consciousness, but in order to develop that of a human being on earth it is necessary for a being to descend to this earth and for a number of incarnations to be embodied in dense matter.'

The soul of the ancient Indian further realized that whatever infinitely higher perfections than man on the earth these spiritual beings possessed, there was one thing they had not in their world, namely the human 'I' consciousness; that to say 'I' as an individual does was not natural in those higher worlds. The Indian felt himself to originate from these realms and everything existing in the spiritual worlds to be summed up for him in his human 'I' consciousness. He knew that to speak of a human 'I' consciousness in the spiritual world had neither meaning nor content. Hence only a word which excludes this 'I' can be applied to everything that in a spiritual sense is spread out in the surrounding world, a word which is not in contact with the 'I'. And the Indian consciousness named that which spread itself out externally the 'Tat', the 'That' in contradistinction to the 'I'. In order to express the fact that man is of the same nature and essence as the 'That', the 'Tat', or the 'It'—that the 'I' or ego had only developed because of the descent to Earth—the Indian said: 'I am Tat, Thou art That.' Thus man's relationship to the surrounding spiritual world (to this clairvoyant penetration of the ultimate nature of our world) was combined in the words: 'It exists; but thou thyself art that.'

But the ancient Indian realized at the same time that the reality without, designated as 'Tat', is also to be found by a man looking into his own inner being, that this reality manifests at one time from without, at another time from within. Therefore people of those ancient times knew that by sinking down into the soul they came to the same primordial spiritual reality as the external 'Tat', but that the right relationship between them and what was living within them as their original 'cause', so to speak, veiled by the life of the soul, was expressed by saying instead of 'Thou art That', 'I am Brahman', and 'I am the All'. And they took the two together to mean the following: 'When I look out into the world of "Tat" I find a spiritual world, and if I dip down into my own soul life I find a spiritual world, and the two are one.'

As we have seen, in ancient India, a perception of the unity of the outer and of the inner was the typical outlook of the soul; and it is to be expected that the other extreme will consist in turning the gaze outwards, and in penetrating through the tapestry of the sense world to the spiritual world lying hidden behind it. And this is what actually happened to a different people. They saw the outer spiritual world, but could not realize immediately that it was the same as the inner spiritual world. Hence it is not surprising that religious conceptions and philosophical thoughts spring up, all fervently directed to the gods and spirits behind the sense world; that mythical and other descriptions for these divine spiritual beings behind the tapestry of the sense world were given to the people; and that in the mysteries of that age people were led into the spiritual world which is behind the sense world. Nor will it be a matter for wonder that side by side with such mysteries and such racial gods something else is to be found, that at the same time there were mysteries leading man along the path through the inner soul life to its deepest foundations. And in very fact we find a region of post-Atlantean civilization where those two kinds of mysteries existed contemporaneously—a region where on the one side the so-called Apollonian culture and mysteries were developed, and on the other the culture and mysteries of Dionysos. Such a division is to be found in ancient Greece. There we have on the one hand the path which was shown to the people as well as to the initiates, the path leading out into the spiritual world, to what is behind the senses, to the spiritual world behind the sun. So far as the Greek knew this world, he gave it the name of the realm of the Apollonian beings. Apollo, the sun god, was the representative of the divine-spiritual beings which exist behind the tapestry of the sense world. But there was also a class of mysteries pointing the way through the soul life into its spiritual foundations, mysteries concerning which we already know that man may enter them only after careful preparation and after having attained a certain degree of maturity. For this reason, the second kind of mysteries was more carefully guarded against immaturity than were the Apollonian. The Apollonian gods were indicated to the masses of the people, whereas the spiritual beings to be found along the path through the inner nature were reserved for those who, through spiritual, intellectual and moral training of their inner life had reached a certain state of maturity. This second kind of mystery cult was known as the Dionysian mystery and its central spiritual being was Dionysos. So it is natural that in Dionysos, this central figure of the inner circle of gods, people perceived a being standing in near and intimate relationship to the human soul—a being not unlike man, but one who did not descend so far as the physical plane, a being to be found by sinking from the physical plane into the depths of the soul life. Here we have in point of fact the deeper causes of the Apollonian and the Dionysian division in the spiritual culture of the Greeks.

In more modern times a dim consciousness that something of the kind had existed in Greece made its appearance in several places. The group gathering round Richard Wagner realized the existence of something of the kind although without definite knowledge of its spiritual foundations. And Friedrich Nietzsche, a member of this group, founded his first remarkable and inspired work, *The Birth of Tragedy out of the Spirit of Music*, on this very division of Greek spiritual life into the Apollonian and Dionysian mystery cults. These occurrences were a dim realization of what may be known to an ever-increasing degree through spiritual meditation. In the minds of many people today there is a kind of yearning for such a deepening of the spiritual life. There is a widespread feeling that this deepening alone can give an answer to man's yearning. Thus in ancient Greece these two divine spiritual worlds are side by side. In ancient India they appeared as a unity, in a state of reciprocal permeation.

Now let us turn again to evolution. We have already seen that only the most advanced group of the northern stream of nations, namely the ancient Persian civilization of Zoroaster, could originate the ideal of creating a body in which the spiritual being approaching humanity and the earth from outside could incarnate. And Zarathustra took upon himself the task of passing through his incarnations in such a way as to take later rebirth in a body spiritualized to such a degree that it was able to receive into itself the sublime Sun Spirit in its most perfect form, in its Christ form. Zarathustra was reborn as Jesus, having made himself ripe through his various incarnations to be the vehicle of the Sun Spirit for the space of three years.

We may now ask: What is the relation of Apollo to the Christ? When a Greek uttered the name of Apollo, he referred to the spiritual realm behind the sun. But people's conception of a being or of a fact differs according to their capacities. The individual who has cultivated a rich inner life within his soul is capable of seeing in a truer form things which a less developed person also sees, so when the Greek uttered the name of Apollo he was indeed referring to the Being which later was revealed as the Christ, but he could only conceive of it in a kind of veiled form, as Apollo. Apollo is in a certain sense a garment of the Christ, resembling in its form the Being within it. Veil after veil had to fall from that figure conceived of by the soul as Apollo before the Christ could become visible and intelligible to the intuition of mankind. Apollo is an intimation of the Christ, but not the Christ Himself.

Now what is the most essentially characteristic quality of the Christ so far as our cycle of evolution is concerned? To consider all those divine-spiritual beings to which people of ancient times looked up to as the upper gods behind the tapestry of the sense world, as the rulers and lords of the spheres and functions of the universe, is to realize that their characteristic quality is that they do not descend so far as the physical plane; they only become visible to the consciousness of the seer, which transcends the physical plane and is able to see on the etheric plane. There Zeus, Apollo, Mars, Wotan, Odin, Thor, who are all real beings, became visible. It was characteristic of these spiritual beings not to descend so far as the physical plane but at the most to manifest temporarily in some kind of physical embodiment, a fact which is cleverly indicated in the myths when mention is made of momentary appearances of Zeus or other gods in human or some other form when they descended to the world of mankind in order to carry out some purpose. It is not permissible to speak of a permanent physical incarnation of these spiritual beings which are behind the sense world. We may say that Apollo is a figure incapable of descending into physical incarnation. For this descent requires a higher power than Apollo possessed, namely the Christ power. And in the Christ all the qualities of the other beings out in the universe were united, all the qualities which are revealed to the consciousness of the seer; but above and beyond all these He possessed the ability to break through the barrier separating the world of the gods from the world of man, and was able to descend into a physical body and become man in a human physical body that had been prepared for Him upon the earth. In the divine spiritual world this ability was possessed by the Christ alone. Thus one being, and one being only of the divine-spiritual world descended so far as the stage of taking up its abode in a human body in the sense world, and living as man among other human beings. This is the great and mighty Christ event, and this is how we have to conceive it. Whereas therefore all gods and spirits can be found only by the consciousness of the seer and beyond the physical world, the Christ is to be found within the physical world, although He is a being of the same nature and essence as the other divine-spiritual beings. The other gods can only be found in the external universe: the Christ is He who was born within the human soul, who, as it were, leaves the outer world of the gods and enters into the inner nature of man. This has been an event of great significance in the evolution of the world and humanity.

Before the Christ event, if an inner god was sought it had been necessary to descend to the sub-terrestrial gods hidden behind the veil of soul experiences; however the Christ is a God who may be found without as well as within. This is the essence of what happened in the fourth post-Atlantean epoch, after the Indian, the Persian and the Egyptian periods. The contemplative vision and abstract perception in ancient India of the fact that the divine-spiritual world was a unity, and that Tat and Brahman, streaming to the soul from two sides, were a unity, became a living life through the Christ event. Formerly people could say that the divinity to be found on the outward path and the divinity to be found on the inward path were one. After the Christ event it was possible to say that if the soul participates in the Christ, a descent to the inner life will reveal a being which is Apollo and Dionysos united in one.

Another question arises here. We have seen that divine-spiritual beings of the external world are, for man, represented by the mightiest of them, by the Christ, who as an outer being at the same time becomes an inner being. But what of those other beings designated in the last lecture as 'luciferic'? Knowledge gained as the result of spiritual development teaches us that it would not be correct to say that the beings under the leadership of Dionysos work themselves through into the human soul life, and that, as it were from the other side, a Dionysos—a luciferic being—

incarnated as a man. Here we arrive at something vitally and essentially connected with the evolution of humanity and of the universe. If we go back to very ancient times, we find that the soul looking outwards sees the external spiritual world, and looking inwards sees the inner divine-spiritual world— the Apollonian world objectively, and the Dionysian world subjectively, to use the Greek expressions. Later on in evolution matters change somewhat. In the most ancient times, when a vast majority of people were possessed of spiritual vision, facts were as I have just described them. Objectively the upper gods were seen, subjectively, the lower gods; and there were these two paths into the spiritual world. In later times man's capacity for spiritual vision decreased; he gradually lost his original dim clairvoyance. But let us take a period in which a few people still possessed a natural spiritual vision. We need not go so very far back, for in the Egypto-Chaldean epoch such natural sight still existed. At that time people, on penetrating through the tapestry of the sense world, saw the upper gods and, on descending into the depths of their own souls, the lower gods. Those who had passed through a certain degree of initiation felt these impressions more clearly and powerfully. I should mention of course that at all times there have existed initiates with full knowledge of the unity of these two worlds; but they are people who have reached the apex of humanity. Centuries therefore before the appearance of Christ on earth, there were people who still had the old spiritual sight, and initiates who by following one path were able to find the upper gods or, following the other, were led to the lower gods. But there came an age where the region which we call the world of the lower gods gradually withdrew from human life and was difficult of attainment even for those who had passed through the early degrees of initiation; but in this period it was comparatively easy at an early stage of initiation to attain to what we call the upper gods behind the outer world of the senses. Take, for instance, an initiate of the ancient Hebrew people. Such an initiate could, even if he had not attained a very high degree of initiation, look into a region where Jehovah was not merely an idea, a concept, but an etheric reality, a being which spoke to them as a man in their spiritual consciousness.

While therefore the existence of Jehovah was proclaimed to the people, to the initiates he was a reality. On the other hand, it had become more difficult for an initiate of the ancient Hebraic world to find anything by dipping down into his own soul life and searching there for the domain of the lower gods. In that region he would have felt no solid ground, but everywhere would have encountered the thick crust of his soul life through which he could not penetrate to the lower gods. The lower gods had withdrawn into a certain unknown obscurity. This was the time of the Christ's descent to the earth, when the luciferic spirits had to a certain extent withdrawn into the darkness. And at that time people in the outer world only knew that the mysteries existed, and that those initiated into them acquired the faculty of penetrating through the forces of the soul life into the Dionysian world. There was just a vague inkling of the deep secrets which could be investigated by man in the mysteries. But the subject was merely alluded to and very few people had a clear idea of it at the time when the Christ was expected. Their ideas of the outer gods were much more definite. There were many people who still had living experience of these gods. But the evolution of humanity progresses. And with what result? There is a history of outer humanity, and in the future there will also be a history of the mysteries. Outer humanity will transform its spiritual culture and the Christ will enter into it more and more. In the mysteries, too, the nature of the Christ Being, which today is hardly appreciated at all, will come to be understood. The God who could be perceived at the time of Zarathustra when spiritual sight was directed to the sun, and who descended to the earth, will be understood with ever-growing intimacy by the human soul. The God who was the ruler of the outer world will become more and more an inner God. The Christ traverses the world in such a way that from a cosmic God who descended upon earth, He becomes an inner mystical God, whom man will gradually be able to experience in the depths of his soul life. Therefore it was that at the time of the descent of the Christ there could be accomplished what His disciples, the Apostles, described in the words: 'We have laid our hands in His wounds, and have heard His words on the mountain.' The essential point is that the Christ was on earth in a physical body. At that time, He could not have been experienced physically within, or understood in His Dionysian nature. He had first to be experienced as the outer, historical Christ. But the progress of man's consciousness of the Christ consists in His ever deeper descent into the soul, and it will become possible for man to live through his own soul experiences subjectively, finding the mystical Christ within his own soul, in addition to the knowledge he has of the outer Christ. It will be observed how in the so-called mysticism which arose in the early days of Christianity, through Dionysius the Areopagite, a friend and pupil of St Paul, the Christ is first understood by external occult faculties. And all the descriptions of this first occult Christian school are of a kind that depict the Christ essentially as having those qualities which he unfolds in the external worlds, and which may be experienced by instinctive spiritual sight when it is turned outwards.

Then let us proceed a few centuries further in human evolution and see what has come about; let us enquire into medieval mystical development, into the deep inner experiences of Meister Eckhart, of Johannes Tauler, etc., and to our more modern mystics. Here are people who look down into their own souls. Just as in ancient times people looked within themselves in order to penetrate through this inner life to Dionysos, so the more modern mystics, piercing inwards, could say like Meister Eckhart: 'The historical Christ is in very truth a fact; His development takes place in outer history but there is a possibility of descending into one's own inward life, and of there finding the inner mystical Christ.' Thus the human soul developed the capacity of finding the Christ not only in the outer world, but also within, of finding the mystical Christ in His Dionysian nature. First the historical Christ came into being, and then through the work of the historical Christ influences were brought to bear on the human soul of such a nature that a mystical Christ within human evolution has become possible. Therefore we may, with regard to modern times, speak of an inner mystical experience of the Christ; but we must also understand that the Christ was a cosmic God before His descent upon earth. If, in those former times, man plunged into his inner soul life, he found not Christ, but Dionysos. Today, if development has come about in the right way, we find an inner Christ Being there.

The Christ, at first a divinity external to the soul, has become a divinity within the soul, who will take fuller possession of it the more the soul experiences draw near to the Christ. Here we have an example of a transformation of principles during the development of the world. When modern people speak of the mystical Christ within the soul they should not forget that everything in the world has developed, and that mystical consciousness has not been the same through all time but has also evolved to its present state. When the Holy Rishis of antiquity looked up into the spiritual worlds they spoke of Vishvakarman, who was the same cosmic being to whom Zoroaster referred when he spoke of Ahura Mazda. It was the Christ Being. Today this being may also be found in the inner life as the mystical Christ. This is the result of the Christ's own deed on the earth. This is the true relation of the cosmic, astronomical Christ to the mystical Christ. The outer god has gradually become an inner god.

But since every event in the external physical world is an effect of a spiritual occurrence, this penetration of the soul by the Christ has also its effect upon the other life. This effect will manifest first of all in the mysteries, and has already partly done so since the foundation of the western mystery schools of the Rosicrucians. When by means of the discipline of the old mystery schools an individual had sunk more deeply into his soul and descended to the lower gods he found Dionysos, which is only another name for the world of the luciferic gods. But at the time when the Christ in His glory was approaching the earth the luciferic reality sank into darkness even for spiritual consciousness, if the latter had not attained the very highest stages. Only the highest initiates were still able to descend to the luciferic gods. Other people had to be told that if they descended while yet unpurified and immature these luciferic beings would only appear in distorted images, as wild demons who would tempt them to all sorts of evil. This is the origin of all the terrible descriptions of this subterranean realm, and of the fear at a certain time of the mere name of Lucifer. And as everything is transmitted hereditarily to persons who do not progress with evolution there are still some who have inherited the fear of the name of Lucifer. But for spiritual consciousness the luciferic world emerges again after the Christ principle has for some time been working in the soul. As soon as the Christ has worked in the soul for a while, the soul, permeated by the Christ substance, becomes mature enough to penetrate again into the realm of the luciferic beings. The Rosicrucian initiates were the first to be able to do this. They strove to understand and see the Christ in such a form that as the mystical Christ He permeated their souls, lived within them, and this Christ substance in their inner being became a bulwark of strength against all attacks. It became a new light within them, an inner, astral light. Historical experience of the Christ in His true being illuminates the soul to such an extent that people again become able to penetrate into the realm of Lucifer. At first only the Rosicrucian initiates were capable of this, and they will gradually carry into the world what they have been able to experience with regard to the luciferic principle, and will pour out over the world that mighty spiritual union which consists in the fact that the Christ, who has poured Himself as substance into the human soul, is understood henceforth through a new influx of the luciferic principle by means of the spiritual faculties that mature in the spirit of individual people.

Let us consider an initiate of the Rose Cross. He first prepares himself by the continual direction of the feeling, conceptions and thoughts within his soul to the great central figure of the Christ, by allowing the mighty figure of the Christ, as depicted by the Gospel of St John, to work upon him, and in this way he purifies and ennobles himself. For our souls change fundamentally when we gaze in reverence upon the figure depicted by the Gospel of St John. If we receive within us what streams forth from this figure, as described by St John, the mystical Christ comes to life within us. And if we further this process by the study of other Christian documents the soul is gradually permeated by the spiritual substance of the Christ, is cleansed and purified and reaches higher worlds. Feelings more especially are purified in this way. We either, like Meister Eckhart and Tauler, learn to conceive of the Christ in a universal sense or else to experience Him with the tenderness of Suso and others; we feel united with that which streamed to the earth through the Christ event from the wide expanse of the heavenly worlds. Thereby a person makes himself ready to be led as a Rosicrucian initiate consciously into those regions which in ancient times were called the Dionysian worlds and may now be called the luciferic worlds.

What is the effect upon modern Rosicrucian initiates of this introduction into the luciferic worlds? If their feelings glow with enthusiasm for the divine as soon as they are permeated with the Christ substance, the other faculties through which we understand the world are illuminated and strengthened by the luciferic principle. In this way the Rosicrucian initiate ascends to the luciferic principle. His spiritual faculties are intensified and elaborated through initiation, so that he not merely feels the Christ mystically within His soul but can also describe Him, can speak of Him and picture Him in spiritual images or thought pictures. So the Christ is not merely dimly felt and experienced but stands before him in concrete outlines, as a figure of the outer sense world. It is possible for man to experience the Christ as soul substance when he directs his gaze to that figure of the Christ which meets him in the Gospels. But to describe and understand Him in the way that other phenomena and events in the world are understood, and thereby to gain an insight into His greatness, His significance and His causative connection with world evolution, is only possible when the Christian initiate advances to knowledge of the luciferic realms.

Thus in Rosicrucian science it is Lucifer who gives us the faculty for describing and understanding the Christ.

What the centuries have been able to do is to propagate the Gospels; so that the Word streaming forth from them enabled hearts and souls to be warmed by their message, to be permeated by the fire and enthusiasm which flow out from them. Today we stand at a stage of human evolution when it can no longer suffice to receive the Gospels as a tradition in the old way; today people need something else. Those who decline to accept this new teaching will have to bear the karma of opposition to the introduction of the luciferic principle into the interpretation of the Gospels. There may be many who say: 'We are content to accept the Gospels as simple Christians; we feel that they satisfy us. The Christ speaks through them, and He does so even when we receive them as traditionally handed down for centuries in religion.' Although these people may imagine themselves to be good Christians they are in reality enemies of the Christ, who on account of their personal egoism, and because they still feel themselves satisfied by what is offered in the traditional interpretation of the Gospels, would sweep away that which in future will bring Christianity into glory. Those who today believe themselves to be the best Christians are often the most effective exterminators of real Christianity.

Those who today understand the development of Christianity think quite differently. They say that they do not wish to be the egoists who think that the Gospels suffice and assert that they will not have anything to do with abstractions. What spiritual science has to offer is far removed from being an abstract teaching. Real Christians today know that humanity needs something more than the Christianity of the egoists; they realize that the world can no longer be satisfied with the old Gospel tradition, and that the light from Lucifer's kingdom must be thrown upon it. They listen to the teachings proceeding from Rosicrucian schools of initiation, wherein the spiritual faculties have been intensified by the luciferic principle, in order to penetrate more and more profoundly into the Gospels, and these initiates have found the Gospels to be of such infinite depth that it is impossible to imagine that they can ever be exhaustively dealt with. But today the time has already arrived when the Rosicrucians must let their teachings flow out into the world; they are called upon to spread abroad what they have gained from the luciferic world in the form of intensification of spiritual forces and faculties, and to pour this into the Gospels. The spiritual science of the West consists in letting the light which streams forth and may be gained from Lucifer's kingdom be cast upon the Gospels. Spiritual science should be an instrument for the interpretation of the Gospels. So it is part of our work to bring to man the joyful message about the substance of the Christ Being, which permeates the world, and to allow the light which may be gained in Lucifer's kingdom on the path of Rosicrucian initiation to fall upon the Gospels. Thus we see that the Christ, who formerly was a God living in the outer world, became the mystical Christ, and that by His ennoblement of the human soul He has brought it back again to the realm called in ancient times the Dionysian world, which for a time had to be shut off and which will be reattained in the future by man. The interpretation of the Christ by spiritual faculties illuminated by Lucifer is the inner and essential kernel of the spiritual stream which must flow through the western channel. And what I have said represents the mission of Rosicrucianism in the future.

What is it therefore that comes to pass in human evolution? Christ and Lucifer, the one as a cosmic god and the other as a god within the human soul, dwelt side by side in ancient times, one to be found in the upper regions and the other in the nether regions. Then the evolution of the world progressed and for some time it was known that Dionysos or Lucifer was far away from the earth. On the other hand, the cosmic Christ was felt to be penetrating the earth to a greater and greater degree; Lucifer again became visible, and was once more able to be known. The paths taken by these two divine spiritual beings may be pictured more or less in the following way. They approached the earth from two different sides. Lucifer became invisible at the time when his path cut across that of the Christ—his light was overpowered by the Christ light. The Christ entered the human soul, became the planetary spirit of the earth, growing more and more to be the mystical Christ within human souls, and can be felt and realized through inner experiences. In this way the soul becomes gradually more capable of again beholding the other being, who took the reverse way, from within to without.

Lucifer, from a being within man's inner nature, a purely earthly being such as he was when he was sought in the mysteries leading to the underworld, becomes a cosmic god. He will appear in ever greater radiance in the outer world which we behold when we look through the tapestry of the sense world. Man's vision will become reversed. In the past Lucifer was seen behind the veil of the inner soul world, and the Christ, as by Zarathustra, behind the veil of the sense world. But in the future the Christ will to an ever greater degree be realized by inner spiritual meditation and Lucifer will be found when the gaze is directed outwards into cosmic regions. Thus we have to record a complete reversal of the conditions by which man can acquire knowledge in the course of human evolution. The Christ, an erstwhile cosmic God, has become an earthly God, who is henceforth the soul of the earth; Lucifer, an erstwhile earthly god, has become a cosmic god. And when in the future man desires again to ascend to the external spiritual world hidden behind the veil of the sense world, and is not willing to stop short at the external and material, he must penetrate through the sense world into the spiritual world and must allow himself to be borne to the light by the 'Light Bringer'. No faculties for penetration into that region can arise in man if he does not create them out of the forces flowing to him from Lucifer's kingdom. People would be drowned in the sea of materialism, would persist in the belief that there is nothing except the outer world of matter, if they did not ascend to Inspiration through the luciferic principle. Just as the Christ principle exists to strengthen our inner being, so the luciferic principle intensifies and develops those faculties by means of which we have to penetrate into the spiritual worlds fully and completely.

Lucifer will intensify our understanding and comprehension of the world; the Christ will strengthen us perpetually within.

LECTURE 7

The Luciferic Influence in History

29 August 1909

There are certain facts in the evolution of mankind which are hardly noticed in outer life. As a result there is misunderstanding of much that is being fulfilled in the spiritual depths underlying human evolution. It has been shown that the mystical Christ experience—such an experience as someone may have when by profound, inner life he permeates his soul experiences with what we have called the Christ substance—was not always possible, but became so in the course of time. The historical descent into incarnation of the Christ was a necessity in preparation for the presence of the mystical Christ in the soul. It is not correct to say that in pre-Christian times the mystical Christ experience had always been possible. Individuals such as Meister Eckhart and other similar personalities with their inner mystical experiences are only possible in the Christian epoch; such experiences would not have been possible at an earlier time. Abstract thinking will be fundamentally unable to understand this; only concrete and spiritually realistic thinking dealing with facts would find its way to these things. Again, the description of the luciferic beings and the Christ can only be comprehensible if we assume that a change took place in the whole human organization—a change, it is true, not to be realized by the external senses or the outer reason, but none the less a radical change. This was accomplished during the last thousand years before the appearance of Christ and during the centuries following His appearance. Since the Atlantean catastrophe man has essentially changed. Notwithstanding that when man incarnates in the present cycle of humanity the important thing is that he depends for his perception of the world, so far as his outer experiences are concerned, upon the instruments which are at his disposal in the envelopes of the physical, etheric and astral bodies, the nature of his perception and realization through subsequent epochs depends upon the changes which this organization undergoes. There is no such thing as a conception of the world which holds good for all times. Man's perception of the world is conditioned by his organization.

Now let us call up before our minds the most radical change in the nature of man that has occurred since the Atlantean catastrophe. Before that the different members of our human nature were connected otherwise than they grew to be later. The etheric body did not cooperate with the physical body during the Atlantean era in the way it has done since. Formerly the etheric body of the head, for instance, extended further above the physical head, and the progress of evolution is expressed by the very fact that the etheric and physical bodies grew more alike and their connection grew closer and closer. Now it is in the etheric body that all the forces necessary for the organization of the physical body reside, all those forces which unite the members of the physical body and produce harmony between them. In the humanity of Atlantis, the forces of the etheric body and especially of the head worked at the building of the physical body from outside. Later these forces withdrew into the space filled by the physical body, and at the present time work more in man's inner being, animating and stimulating it. However this was only a matter of development.

If we wish to understand the old Indian culture we must clearly realize that the conditions were quite different from what they became during the Egypto-Chaldean epoch. And then in humanity of the Graeco-Roman epoch there was such a complete permeation of the physical body by the etheric

body that clairvoyant consciousness would not have perceived the etheric body extending far beyond the physical
body in any part of the human organization. This had not
been the case with the ancient Indians. Their clairvoyant
vision perceived the etheric body still extending, especially as
regards the head, out beyond the physical body. Hence a
native of old India saw the world quite otherwise than did a
native of old Egypt. Someone belonging to the Graeco-
Roman people saw the world much as it is to be seen today,
i.e. as a sense-tapestry of colours, shades, etc. But the whole
of this world which lies spread out before present-day sense-
perception was to the Indian spirit of olden times finely
permeated by what we might today call the misty cloud
characteristic of etheric nature. It arose from all things, so
that they looked as if they were burning, and a fine misty
smoke arose out of each form. The manner of perceiving
then was what might be called a seeing of the etheric element,
which was spread out over everything like dew or hoar frost.
That peculiar kind of sight was then normal; at the present
time the human soul can only attain to it by means of special
exercises given by spiritual science.

The object of the progressive evolution of mankind
through the different periods of civilization is to cause the
etheric body to descend deeper and deeper into the physical
body. Thus the whole manner of human perception changes,
for all human perception depends upon the way in which the
etheric body is organized. And this in its turn is connected
with the fact that the luciferic beings manifesting within the
earth and within the soul have risen to the state of cosmic
beings, and that the Christ Being who was formerly a cosmic
being descended into incarnation in a human body and has
now become an inner being.

This permeation of the Apollonian with the Dionysian
principle—this transposition, as it were—only became possible because of a corresponding change in the human

organization. It was a change that not only affected the past but was also a preparation for the future. We live in a time when the most complete inner permeation of the physical by the etheric body is already a thing of the past—a time when the tendency of evolution is in the opposite direction. We live in an era in which the etheric body is slowly emerging from the physical body. The normal development of humanity will in the future consist in the gradual emergence of the etheric body from the physical body. The time will come when the human organization will once again wear the appearance which it wore in grey primeval ages, and we shall again see the etheric body spreading out beyond the human physical body. We are in the middle of this transition, and many of the more subtle diseases characteristic of the present time would be understood if this were known. But all this has a meaning and corresponds with great cosmic laws, for man could not attain the goal of his evolution unless he thus underwent a transposition of the constituent parts of his organization. Now everything within us is permeated by our whole surroundings, and by the divine spiritual beings in the spiritual world sending their currents down into us, just as the physical elements of the earth send their currents into our physical organization. At the time when the etheric body was outside the physical body, currents were perpetually pouring into this etheric body; man experienced this consciously then as a cosmic revelation, as something revealed to him inwardly. These currents descending into his etheric body from the spiritual world also worked at the perfecting of his physical body.

Now, that which descended into the etheric body of man and was experienced as the most inward element of his being was the influence of the luciferic world, a great and powerful inheritance brought over from the old ages of the pre-Atlantean evolution. The fact that these luciferic influences had become so much darkened that man, at the very time when Christ appeared, could perceive nothing of them unless he had reached a high grade of initiation is explained by the fact that the etheric body drew more and more inside the physical body and became one with it; and man learned to make increasing use of the physical organs as instruments. It was therefore necessary that the divine-spiritual being shortly to appear on earth should be manifest on the physical plane as a figure able to be perceived physically, should incarnate like other physical beings upon the earth. Only thus could mankind have at that time understood a god appearing in a body because it had become accustomed to consider true only what could be observed by means of the instrument of the human physical body. This had to come to pass before those who surrounded the Christ could say by way of emphasizing an event, 'We have placed our hands in His wounds, and our fingers in the imprints of the nails.' This certainty yielded by the senses had to live as a feeling in those men, a feeling which gave the stamp of truth to the event. To that sort of testimony a man of the old Indian age would have attached no importance; he would have said: 'The spiritual perceived by means of the senses means nothing much to me; in order to realize the spiritual there must be ascent to a certain grade of clairvoyant cognition.' Understanding of Christ therefore had gradually to be developed like everything else in the world.

However, the luciferic impulse which man formerly had in his etheric body gradually became exhausted. That which he had brought with him out of primeval ages when his etheric body did not as yet dwell entirely in the physical body, but was still outside and received the luciferic influence through the portion that still was outside, was gradually used up. In order that the etheric body might slip into the physical body it had to lose the capacity of realizing the higher worlds through its etheric organs. So, at a certain epoch it is true to say of our human ancestors that they were still able to see into the spiritual worlds, and what they saw is preserved in their literature. There was, as it were, a primeval wisdom. The reason why later this was not more directly attainable was that as the etheric body was taken up into the physical body man could only make use of his physical senses and of his physical reason. Clairvoyant power was paralysed. The faculty of seeing into the spiritual world was therefore only possible in the initiates who ascended to the supersensible worlds by means of systematic training.

The reverse process is now being enacted. Mankind is entering a condition in which the etheric body is to a certain extent drawing itself out of the physical body again. But it must not be thought that it now receives spontaneously everything which in earlier times it possessed as an ancient heritage. If nothing else happened but its withdrawal, the etheric body of man would just leave the physical body and would retain in itself none of the forces which it formerly possessed. In the future it will be born from out of the human physical body. If the human physical body did not add something to it, this etheric body would be empty, barren. The future of human evolution will be that people will, as it were, allow their etheric body to leave their physical bodily nature, and they will eventually have the possibility of being able to send it out empty. What does that mean? The etheric body is the force-bearer, the energizer of all that takes place in the physical body. It must not only provide forces for the physical body when it is entirely concealed within it, but at all times; it must provide forces for the physical body even when it is again partly outside it. If the etheric body is left empty it cannot react upon the physical body, for it would then have no strength with which to react. The etheric body must, after it has passed through the physical body, have obtained its forces from within the physical body. The forces with which the etheric body can react again upon the physical body must have been drawn from within the latter. The task of present-day humanity is to absorb into itself that which can only be acquired through activity in a physical body. That which is gained within the physical body accompanies evolution, and when in future incarnations man lives in organisms wherein the etheric body is to a certain extent released from the physical body he will experience in his consciousness a kind of memory through the partially liberated physical body.

Now let us ask ourselves: What enables the physical body to hand something on like an heirloom to the etheric body? What enables a person to send such forces into his etheric body that someday he will be in a position to bear an etheric body itself and able to send back certain forces into the physical body from outside? Suppose man's life, let us say from 3000 BC to our own era and on to AD 3000 had been such that nothing more was added to him than what would have been his without the coming of Christ; he would then have experienced in his physical body nothing that might bestow a power on the etheric body when it is released from the physical body. That which a man can hand on is what he can gain within the physical world through the Christ event. All association with the Christ principle and the experiences we may have in connection with the appearance of Christ sink down into the life of the soul in the physical world, and the soul as well as all that is physical are prepared in such a way that there can flow into the etheric body that which it will need in the future. Therefore the Christ event had to take place, to permeate the human soul in order that mankind should be able to understand its future evolution. That which is in the physical body today sends out forces into the etheric body; and the etheric body, nourished by the physical experiences of the Christ, will take up these forces in order again to become clairvoyant and possess the life forces which will sustain the physical body in the future. Hence what man experiences of Christ through the reversal of the principles has its proper bearing upon the future of human evolution.

But this alone would not suffice. By passing through the Christ experience in our own souls, by becoming more and more familiar with the Christ, and by letting Him grow more and more into our soul experiences we do indeed thus influence the etheric body, and pour streams of force into it. Now if this etheric body withdraws and enters into a wrong element it will undoubtedly have the Christ force, but if it does not meet there the forces which are able to work in a sustaining and enlivening way upon the Christ principle, which has entered it, it will find itself in a sphere in which it cannot live. The outer forces would destroy it. It would, being permeated with the Christ, and having entered an unsuitable element, be faced with its own destruction, and would react destructively upon the physical body. Furthermore the etheric body must make itself fit once more to receive the light out of which it originally sprang forth, the light from the realm of Lucifer. Whereas by an inner experience man formerly saw Lucifer appear through the veil of his soul life, he must now prepare himself to be able to experience Lucifer as a cosmic being in the world around him. From having been a sub-terrestrial god, Lucifer becomes a cosmic god. Man must prepare himself in such a way that his etheric body is provided with such forces as make Lucifer a fructifying and a beneficent element instead of a destructive one. Man has to pass through the Christ experience, but in such a way that he becomes capable of recognizing in this world the spiritual fabric of which the world was created.

Training such as spiritual science offers is fully empowered to prepare the whole nature of man again to understand the light of Lucifer's realm, because only thus can the human etheric body receive life forces adequate to it. Christ was influencing man even before He appeared upon the earth. As long ago as the age when Zarathustra was pointing up to Ahura Mazda, the force of Christ was radiating down. And from the other direction there shone the power of Lucifer.

That is reversed as we have seen; in the future the forces of Lucifer will stream in from outside, while the Christ will dwell within. The human organization must again be influenced from two sides. The old Indian realized on the one side 'That thou art', and on the other side 'I am the All' and knew that the world which he saw outside was the same as that within. In ancient Indian times this was realized as an abstract truth; it will be realized on earth as a concrete experience of the soul when the time is accomplished, when by means of suitable preparation that which was manifest prophetically among the ancient Indians shall come to life again in a new form. Thus does human evolution proceed in the post-Atlantean epoch.

Hence it is clear that the evolution of humanity does not move in a straight line, but runs its course, as does everything in nature. I have given the example of a plant, which grows but cannot develop its fruit unless a new factor comes into its development. Here is a picture which shows that other influences must come in from another side. There is no such thing as an evolution which proceeds along a straight line. The luciferic and the Christ principles had to overlap one another. Those who seek to find an undeviating evolution can never understand the world evolution; only those who notice the divided streams and how they mutually fructify each other can really understand evolution. During the old Indian civilization, when man was in a certain sense differently organized his outlook was different. What man's outlook then was can only be definitely experienced by means of that kind of clairvoyant research which is suitable for the present age. And clairvoyance is a power which today has to be acquired by effort, although it was at one age a natural faculty. It is very difficult indeed, even for those who have a thorough knowledge of spiritual science to understand how much the soul-experiences in the old Indian age differed from those of

later times, and one can only try to clothe this difference in
words which approximate to the real sense.

When a person looks out into the world today he perceives
it through his various senses. We cannot here go into all that
modern science has to say about sense-perception; it will
suffice to hold in our mind the usual conception that man
perceives the outer world by means of his various senses, and
gathers the different impressions together by means of the
spiritual faculty that is bound up with the physical brain.
Think this over a little, and it will become evident that there
is a great difference in the character of the different sense-
perceptions; compare, for instance, the sense of hearing with
that of sight. It is evident that as regards hearing, if we look in
the outer world for the facts corresponding to it, we find
matter in movement, air in regular motion. If our instrument
of hearing is brought into contact with this air which is in
motion we experience what is called hearing. But the inner
experience of hearing and the air in motion without are two
very different things. Now sight is not such a simple thing as
hearing, though physicists have made it appear to be so.
Their postulation, built up by analogy, runs somewhat as
follows. Let us take, they say, one of the finer substances
which moves just as does the air outside. But the realistic
thinker sees a great difference, namely that as regards the ear
one can very easily detect what moves outside. It can easily be
proved that something really does move outside—as far as
the ear is concerned—by putting little paper riders on a violin
string and striking it. But nobody can see for himself the
existence of vibrations in the ether. It is a hypothesis; it exists
only as a theory of physics and is non-existent for the realistic
thinker. Sense-perception by means of sight is a very different
thing. What is perceived through light is much more objective than what is sensed through hearing. We perceive light as
colour, we perceive it spread out in space; but we cannot, as
in the case of sound, go into the outer world in search of

external processes. Such distinctions as these are readily overlooked by man of modern times. The old Indian, possessing a finer consciousness of the whole outer world, could not have overlooked this. He perceived all these delicate external distinctions.

I only want to point out that there are characteristic and essential differences between the realms of the various senses. If we consider the German language it may strike us that with the same word we express an inner soul-experience and an impression that comes, in a sense, from outside (I admit that this happens in incorrect speaking). That word is the word 'feeling'. We speak of the five senses: sight, hearing, smell, taste and touch. When speaking of feeling in a superficial way we mean the sense of touch, but call it feeling and add that which is experienced by this sense to the outer sense-experiences. Again, inspired by the genius of speech, we define in a much more spiritual sense than is generally realized an inner soul-experience by the word 'feeling'. Experiences of joy or pain are defined as feelings. This particular feeling of which we are here speaking is an intimate soul-experience; the other feelings, produced by the sense of touch, are always caused by some external object. The other feeling may be associated with an external object, but it can be seen that an external object is not the only cause, because the effect upon one person is different from the effect upon another. We have two experiences: one connected with the external sense, the other bound to the inner. These two at the present day appear to be widely divided, but this was not always the case. Here we come to another view of what has previously been described in an external sense. We have described how the etheric body slips in and out again. This is connected with the fact that something takes place in the inner being of man. Today these two experiences, the experience of 'feeling' within one and the experience caused by personal contact with an external object which we also describe by the word 'feeling', are widely divided. The further we go back in the evolution of humanity, that is to say, the further the etheric body is outside the physical body, so much the nearer are these two experiences to one another. They are only widely divided in mankind today. In the Indian epoch this difference did not exist to the same extent. At that time the inner experience of feeling and the outer were more like each other. Why was that?

If you meet someone today who has an evil thought about you (let us say you dislike him and he has the same sort of feeling towards you), you will as a general rule, if you are only provided with the external senses and the physical brain, not be deeply aware of his feelings, of his sympathies and antipathies. If he should strike you, you would be aware of it, because your sense of feeling would notice it. In the old Indian times there was a different state of things. Man then was so organized that he was not only aware of that which is felt by the present crude sense of touch, but also of that which today has withdrawn into his inner being; he was still able to sense what someone else felt about him. Through sympathetic comprehension of another individual's feelings he awakened in his soul just such an experience as we have through the sense of touch. He felt the physical-psychical process. On the other hand that which we call our inner feeling was not so far developed in those days; it was still more closely connected with the outer world. Man had his sorrows and joys which in many respects corresponded more to outer happenings; but he could not retire so deeply into his inner being as he can today. At the present time, inner soul-experience is to a far greater extent severed from the whole surroundings than formerly was the case. At the present time a person may find himself in a position in which he is surrounded by circumstances which could be better; but because of his inner soul life being severed from his surroundings he may perhaps feel inward pain without any real cause on account of his way of looking at the world.

This would have been impossible at the time of the old Indian epoch of civilization. At that time the inner impressions were a much truer reflection of what went on in the outer environment, for man's feeling was then to a greater extent bound up with the external world. The reason for this was that in those olden times, for example, man, in his whole make up, stood in a very different relation to light. The light surrounding us has not only its external physical aspect but, like everything physical, is also permeated by soul and spirit. The course of human evolution was such that the soul and spirit of the outer world withdrew more and more from man and gradually the physical part came to be all that was perceptible. Man came to perceive light as a fluid pouring into his organization from all sides, and within this light streaming through him he felt its soul. Today the soul of the light is stopped by the human skin. The Indian organization was permeated by what lives as soul within the light, and man realized the soul of the light. That light was the bearer of what could be perceived as sympathy and antipathy in other beings, which has now withdrawn with the soul of the light away from human beings. This was connected with other experiences. Today when people inhale and exhale they can, at the most, know of the existence of breath through the mechanical working. If it is at all chilled they see it becoming moist. This is a mechanical way of seeing the breath. Improbable as it may appear to the man of today, it is nevertheless true that by means of occult research we can substantiate the fact that most of the old Indians had quite a different conception of what their breath signified. The soul of light had not as yet withdrawn from what went on around people of that time, so that they perceived the air as it was breathed in and breathed out in different light and dark shades of colour. They saw the air pouring in and out again like flames of fire. We may therefore say that even the air itself has become something quite different, by reason of the change that has taken place in man's conceptual life.

Air today is something that is only perceived mechanically by people through the resistance it offers, because they are no longer directly aware of the soul of the light which permeates the air. Man has parted even from this last remnant of instinctive perception. The old Indian would not have called that which is breathed in and out merely 'air'; he would have called it 'fire air', because he saw it in varying degrees of fiery radiations.

There again we have an example of how even in external experiences the transformation in the constitution of man in the course of evolution is manifest. These are intimate, hidden processes in human evolution, and we can never understand the Vedas if we do not understand how and in what sense the words are used. If we read the words contained in them without knowing that they described what could then be seen, the words would lose all sense and our interpretation would be completely wrong. We must always take the realities into consideration when we approach the study of ancient documents. That which lives in the human soul alters in character with the course of time. And now a certain fact will be comprehensible which could not have been so without these statements, statements which are quite independent of any proofs to be established by physical research. Look into the eastern writings and see how the elements are there enumerated. They are placed in the following order: earth, water, fire, air and ether. Only in Greek times do we find a different order which to us today is the obvious one and upon which we base all our understanding, namely earth, water, air, fire and the other ethers. Why is this so? The old Indian consciousness saw, just as man sees today, what is manifested through the solid (that which we call the earth), through the fluidic, or water, to speak in the spiritual sense. But what we today call air to the old Indians was fire, for they still saw the fire in the air—they described what they saw as fire. We no longer see this fire in the air; we only feel it as heat. Everything has changed since the fourth post-Atlantean epoch. So it was that only when they went a little higher in the series of the elements the Indians came to an element in which at that time there appeared to mankind what we today call air—the air to us being penetrated by light, but not revealing the light. In respect to fire and air, man's vision has been entirely reversed. What we have said about Christ and Lucifer crossing each other—that Christ the cosmic being has entered within the human soul, while Lucifer who at first was within man has become a cosmic being—holds good in all departments of life. That which in the first post-Atlantean epoch was what we call fire is at the present day perceivable as air, and that which we today see as fire was then seen as air. That which underlies human evolution is expressed not only in great things but also in small ones. These things must not be put down to chance; we can see into the profundities of what happens in the course of the evolution of mankind if we look at things from the only real point of view, that of spiritual science. The Indian consciousness was one which felt the unity of what lies deep down in the soul with what is outside it; hence the Indian lived to a greater degree in his environment.

The last echoes of what existed in the ancient Indian as instinctive sight are to be found in the rudimentary 'clairvoyance' possessed today by those individuals who have what we call second sight. Suppose when walking along the street anywhere there enters the mind the thought of a certain man whom at the moment we cannot physically see, and we meet him a little further on. Why was the thought of him in the consciousness before he was seen? It is because his influence has entered into the subconsciousness, whence it ascended into the consciousness as a complete thought. Today man possesses in rudimentary form what was once of great significance in his life. In earlier times there existed a much closer connection between inner and outer feeling. These are some more detailed instances of my oft-repeated statements that humanity has evolved out of the old dim clairvoyance into the full consciousness of the senses we now possess, and humanity in the future will once again evolve a fully conscious clairvoyance. This will be attained in such a way that man will consciously experience it; he will know that his etheric body goes forth out of him and that he can use the organs of the etheric body just as he can the physical body.

In earlier, more spiritual ages when people had more wisdom than has modern abstract materialistic science they were always conscious that there was an old clairvoyance to the possessors of which the world became transparent. They felt that man had lost this old sight and had entered into his present state. Formerly, people did not express their knowledge in abstract formulae and theories, but in mighty, vivid pictures. The myths are not 'thought out' or invented, but are the expressions of a profound primeval wisdom acquired by spiritual vision. In ancient times there was consciousness of the fact that at a still earlier epoch man had embraced the whole world in his feeling, and this is expressed in the myths. The 'clairsentience' of the old Indian was the last remnant of an original, dim clairvoyance. This was known; but what was not known was that this clairvoyance— let us summarize it so—withdraws little by little, giving way to the external life which is confined to the world of the senses. The more important myths express this very fact. It was known, for instance, that there were mystery places leading the way to the sub-terrestrial spirits and that there were others leading up to the cosmic spirits. There was a sharp distinction between them. People who were not initiated knew nothing of this, just as today individuals who do not seek along the right paths have no idea that there is such a thing as mystery wisdom. A certain amount of information filtered out. With regard to the mysteries it is true to say that the further we go back into olden times the more significant does their age of splendour appear. Even the Greek mysteries do not belong to the most brilliant period. The mysteries themselves had fallen into decadence.

Nevertheless, the people knew that that which came from those places where clairvoyant consciousness was still active was connected with the spiritual substance which streams through the world and animates it; they knew that where clairvoyant consciousness still prevailed, something could be experienced about the world which was possible in no other way.

And even in the period of their decadence clairvoyant consciousness was cultivated in these oracle-places, and from them information was conveyed to mankind such as cannot be experienced by ordinary sense-methods, and intellectual conceptions bound up with them. Yet it was also known that man is developing, that that which could be attained by the old clairvoyance, useful and practicable in ancient days, was no longer adequate for later times. The Greeks had a deep consciousness of the fact that that which came from the oracles certainly aroused curiosity, that men would fain know something about the hidden connections of the world, but that they had departed from the right method of using such clairvoyant information, that man's relation to the world was different from what it had formerly been and that therefore no good could originate from clinging to the results of the old clairvoyance. This is what the Greeks wanted to express and they did so in magnificent pictures. One such picture is the Oedipus legend. Through an oracle (that is to say, from a place in which secret connections, hidden from the human gaze, were clairvoyantly perceived), the father was told that if a son were born to him disaster would result, that this son would murder his father and marry his mother. This son was born. The father tried to prevent what had been seen clair-voyantly from coming to pass. The son was sent away and brought up in another place, but he came to know the oracle, that is to say, something entered his soul which could only be known by means of clairvoyance. The Greek consciousness would say: Something still continues to enter into man from olden times, but the human organization has already pro-gressed so far that it is no longer adapted to this sort of clairvoyance, and cannot make use of it. Oedipus listens to the oracle, but acts in such a way that it is all the more cer-tainly fulfilled. People can no longer handle the results of clairvoyance; the spiritual world has withdrawn and the old clairvoyance is no longer of service to them. But there has always existed a consciousness that things will one day entirely change and that what comes from spiritual worlds will once again mean something to humanity. People have felt that what comes from these spiritual worlds will be covered over by sense life only for a time. Of these facts consciousness has existed, and has been expressed in the myths by the forces of human evolution which created them. We have seen that the Christ event, when the two forces, the Lucifer principle and the Christ principle, crossed each other, was the decisive one in human evolution. The Christ event was the turning point, when that which comes from out of the cosmos, from the fountain of the spirit, was to be poured as a ferment into human evolution. It had been lost, but it had to be poured in again as a ferment. That which was harmful to mankind, that which made it into something evil, is poured in as a ferment and transformed into good. The evil has to drop into the fructifying spiritual power inherent in human evolution and work with it for the good. That too has been expressed in the myths.

There is another legend which runs somewhat as follows. A certain man and wife were told by an oracle that they would have a son who would bring disaster upon his whole people. This son was to murder his father and marry his mother. This son was born to the mother. On account of the warning, this son was sent away too; he was put upon the island of Kariot and was found by the queen of that island. And because she and her husband had no son she adopted him. But later on a son was born to her. Then the foundling thought he was wrongly treated and he killed the real son. He was obliged to flee from the island of Kariot, and he went to the court of Pilate in Palestine, where he obtained employment as overseer of Pilate's household. He quarrelled with his neighbour, of whom he knew nothing beyond the fact that he was his neighbour. In the course of this quarrel he killed him and later married the widow. Only then did he learn that it was his real father whom he had killed and that it was therefore his mother whom he had married. The story tells us that he saw his entire existence ruined but did not behave like Oedipus, for he was overcome by remorse and went to the Christ and the Christ received him; this was Judas Iscariot, Judas from Kariot. And the evil which dwelt in Judas became a leaven in the whole of evolution. For the deed of Palestine is connected with the betrayal by Judas. Judas is bound up with the whole event; he belongs to the twelve that are not thinkable without him. Here we see that the sayings of the oracle were indeed fulfilled, and further that they are embodied in universal evolution in the form of evil which is transformed and lives on as good.

The story (which is in reality wiser than external science) indicates in the most significant way that there is such a transformation in human nature in the course of time, and that the same thing has to be regarded differently at different epochs. In speaking of the fulfilment of an oracular saying we must not relate it in the same way when speaking of the time of Oedipus as when speaking of the time of Christ. The same fact is at the one period the story of Oedipus; at another, in the time of Christ, it becomes the story of Judas. Only when we know the spiritual facts lying at the foundation of the evolution of the world and of humanity do we understand the results of those spiritual facts which are manifest to external historical conceptions. All phenomena of the sense world, all external sense-impressions or manifestations of the human soul can be comprehended by us when we understand their spiritual basis. That which the investigator of spiritual worlds discovers he gladly hands on as a stimulus to those who are willing to take it from him and who will then examine the external facts which confirm it. If what is discovered in the spiritual world be true, it is confirmed in the physical world. But every true explorer of the spiritual life will say that in communicating his knowledge of the higher world he facilitates and desires the testing of all external facts in the light of his assertions. If what I have said about the reincarnation of Zarathustra for instance be compared with external history, it will be found that what has been said stands every test, if sufficiently careful search is made in external history. External life becomes comprehensible only when there is knowledge of the inner, the spiritual.

LECTURE 8

The Nature of the Luciferic Influence in History

30 August 1909

Up to the present we have given special attention to the way in which the soul of man in the course of evolution approaches and experiences those beings which are either to be taken as belonging to the kingdom of Christ or to the kingdom of Lucifer. We pointed out, for instance, that the way to those cosmic beings which in pre-Christian times had the Christ as their central figure led outwards, but that the way into the kingdom of Lucifer penetrated within the soul, breaking through the veils of the soul itself. And we pointed out how through the appearance of Christ on the earth this has altered in such a way that there has been a transposition of these realms, and that mankind has advanced to an age wherein Christ must be sought within and Lucifer without. In order to establish harmony between various statements already familiar to many readers in regard to the luciferic beings, we must again say a few words about the nature of Lucifer.

Everything in this world is complicated and may be looked at from many different points of view. It will, therefore, sometimes appear as if statements are not always in accord; light must be thrown upon a certain fact sometimes from one side and sometimes from another. Just as it is correct to describe a leaf first from the upper side and then from the lower, while it is one and the same leaf, in the same way do we describe the luciferic principle correctly when as in previous lectures we speak of it by pursuing the path which the soul has to take to encounter this luciferic principle. But naturally one may also consider the evolution of our earth and of the world in general more from a super-terrestrial standpoint, and characterize the position of luciferic beings in the progress of the world from another point of view. We will devote a few words to this subject.

We know that our earth, sun and moon were once one being; that the sun separated itself from the earth in order to be a dwelling place for beings of a higher evolutionary stage, who could then work in upon our earth from outside; that after the withdrawal of the sun from the earth beings of a still higher order remained united with the earth in order to bring about the separation of the moon; and if we think of the fact that the beings who separated the moon from the earth were those who stimulated a new inner life in man, arousing in him a soul life and thus preserving him from mummification we shall soon be able to establish harmony between things already familiar to us and things we have been considering in the preceding lectures. We shall realize that as far as those beings which left the earth with the sun are concerned it is natural that man in his further evolution should find them in the first place by turning his gaze to where they went with the sun. Therefore man had to seek for the realm and activity of the sun beings with all their sub-beings, along the path leading outwards into the world behind the tapestry of sense phenomena. Those beings, however, which to a certain extent were still greater benefactors of mankind and who through the withdrawal of the moon stimulated man's inner soul life had to be sought by descending into man's inner life, into a sub-earthly soul region, in order to find what was hidden from the external sight, and are the sub-terrestrial gods. These are the ones who separated the moon from the earth and aroused the soul life of man. Within the life of the soul was sought the way leading to those gods who were associated with the beneficent event of the withdrawal of the moon. If at first we look only at these two kingdoms, of the sun gods and of the moon gods, we may define the beings as gods to be found outside in the heavens and gods to be found within the soul; and we may designate the way leading out-wards as the sun-path, and the way leading inwards into the soul as the luciferic path. The beings of Lucifer are those who did not participate in the withdrawal of the sun from the earth. And certain other beings, who are the highest bene-factors of mankind but at first had to remain hidden, and who did not accompany the sun in its withdrawal, belonged strictly speaking to neither of those kingdoms. Those were the beings who remained behind during the Old Moon evolution, who did not attain to that grade which as spiritual beings, standing at that time much higher than men on the moon, they might have reached. Thus it was impossible for them to participate in the withdrawal of the sun, during the evolution of the earth which followed. In a certain sense their destiny was to go out, as did the sun spirits, and to work down upon the earth from the sun; but it was not possible for them to do. It therefore came to pass that these beings, in a certain way, made an endeavour to separate themselves from the earth with the sun, but they could not keep pace with the conditions of evolution of the sun and fell back again upon the earth.

These beings, then, did not from the beginning remain behind with the earth when the sun separated from it; they could not exist in the Sun evolution and fell back again to be reunited with the Earth evolution. Now what did these beings do in the course of the Earth evolution? They tried with the help of human evolution upon the earth to continue their own quite individual evolutionary course. They could not approach the human 'I'; and those beings who had brought about the separation of the moon could approach the human 'I' from within. The beings who had fallen back from the sun approached the human soul when it was not yet ripe to receive the revelation to the higher benefactors who had brought about the separation of the moon. They approached the human soul too soon. If man had fully awaited the beneficial influence of those spiritual beings who worked from the moon, that is to say, from the inner part of his being, then that which actually came to pass at an earlier epoch would have come to pass later. These moon gods would have slowly ripened the souls of human beings until a corresponding evolution of the 'I' had become possible. But these other beings approached man and poured their influence not into the 'I' but into the human astral body from within, just as the moon gods do. These beings sought the same way, through the inner being of the soul, upon which later the real moon gods worked; that is to say, these beings settled down in the kingdom of Lucifer. These are the beings which are symbolized in the old biblical writings by the serpent. They are the beings which approached the human astral body too soon and worked in the same manner as all other beings which work from within. And since we designate beings whose influence is from within as luciferic, we include also those beings which remained behind. They came to man when he was still unripe for such an influence; they are on the one hand his seducers, but they also create freedom for him, create the possibility of his astral body becoming independent of those divine beings which would otherwise have taken his 'I' under their protection and would have poured into it all that can be poured into the essence of the 'I' from divine spheres.

Thus these luciferic beings came to the astral body of man and filled it with all that can give him enthusiasm for the sublime, the spiritual; they worked upon his soul and, although they were beings of a higher spiritual order than man, they were in a certain sense his seducers. That which in the course of the evolution of the earth came to man, and which on the one hand brought him freedom and on the other the possibility of evil, came from within, from Lucifer's kingdom. For these beings could not manifest themselves from without; they had to insert themselves into the inner part of the soul, for that which approaches man's 'I' can come from without, but nothing external in this sense can come to his astral body only. In the great kingdom of the Light-bearer, of the beings of Lucifer, there are subspecies of which we can well understand that they might become the seducers of man. And we can also well understand that just on account of these beings strenuous discipline was practised when it was a question of leading man into those realms which lie on the other side of the veil of the soul world; for if he was led along the inner path of the soul he met there not only the good luciferic beings who had given him inner light but also, and first, those luciferic beings who were his seducers and who spurred him on by imparting pride, ambition and vanity to his soul.

It is very important to realize that we should never try to encompass the worlds behind the sense world and behind the soul world with the intellectual concepts of modern culture.

If we speak of the luciferic beings, we must become acquainted with the whole range of their kingdom, with all their species, categories and variations. We should then see that when at times someone mentions the danger of a certain species of luciferic being the speaker is not always aware of the whole extent of the kingdom in question. It may be right to speak of certain species of luciferic beings in the sense of some ancient script, but we must at the same time take into consideration the fact that the reality is infinitely deeper than people can generally realize. At a time when, in people of a certain period of culture, both outward turning and inward turning contemplation were still very keen, man perceived that the outward path led to the realization of 'That thou art' and that the inner path led to the realization of 'I am the All'—that the outer and the inner path both led to the 'I' as a unity. In that first post-Atlantean epoch of civilization man was able to think and feel quite differently about what underlay the spiritual realms than was possible at a later time. It is on that account extraordinarily difficult for ordinary consciousness to transport itself into that wonderful post-Atlantean culture and to identify itself with a soul living at that time.

We have seen how completely different man's feeling life was at that early time, how he felt the soul of the light stream in from all sides through his skin, as it were, and how through this he was able to collect out of the surrounding world experiences which are hidden from him today. But something else was connected with all this.

Those familiar with my *Outline of Occult Science*, will know that human evolution in the post-Atlantean era is divided into the old Indian, the old Persian, the Egypto-Chaldean, the Graeco-Roman, and the present cultural epochs; in the Graeco-Roman period came the Christ event. Our culture epoch will be followed by another and this in its turn by the last, after which the earth will again undergo a change somewhat as it did at the time of the Atlantean catastrophe. We have therefore seven epochs of civilization. In these seven we have a central one standing alone, the Graeco-Roman epoch of civilization with the Christ event. The other epochs of civilization bear a certain relationship to one another. The Egypto-Chaldean civilization repeats itself in certain phenomena of the fifth, i.e. of our own epoch. Certain phenomena, facts and conceptions apparent in the Egypto-Chaldean epoch reappear, but wearing of course a somewhat different form because they are permeated by the intervening Christ impulse. This is not a simple repetition of the Egypto-Chaldean civilization, but a repetition wherein everything is steeped in what the Christ brought to the earth. It is in one sense a repetition and yet in another it is not. Individuals who have had a deeper understanding for the course of human evolution and who have taken part in it with their souls have always felt something of the kind. Many such persons even if they have not advanced to occult knowledge are pervaded by something like a recollection of old Egyptian experiences. The wonderful knowledge of the stars in their courses which the wise men of Egypt brought through into their Hermetic science has revived in our fifth epoch of civilization in another and more material form. And those who participated in the revival felt this with special emphasis. Let me give one example only.

When that individuality who once in the mystery places of Egypt raised the eyes of his soul up to the stars and sought to unravel their secrets in celestial space after the manner of those days, under the guidance of the Egyptian sages, lived again in our own epoch as Kepler, that which had existed in another form in his Egyptian soul appeared in a newer guise as the great laws of Kepler which today are such an integral part of astrophysics. It came to pass also that within the soul of this man there arose something which forced these words to be uttered—words which may be read in the writings of Kepler—'Out of the holy places of Egypt I have brought the sacred vessel; I have transported it to the present time, so that men may understand something in these days of those influences which are able to affect even the most distant future.' We might give hundreds of such examples to show how that which existed in the Egypto-Chaldean epoch of civilization lives over again in a new form.

We are now in the fifth epoch of civilization of the post-Atlantean era. This will be followed by the sixth, which will be very important. It will be a repetition of, and at the same time an advance upon, the old Persian civilization of Zarathustra. Zarathustra looked up to the sun and saw behind the physical sunlight the Christ Spirit whom he called Ahura Mazda, and drew people's attention to Him. This Christ Being has now descended to earth; Christ must penetrate so deeply into the innermost part of those souls who in the course of the sixth period of civilization have made themselves sufficiently ripe that numbers of people on looking into the innermost part of their souls will be able to feel that powerful emotion arise within them which Zarathustra formerly was able to arouse when he pointed to Ahura Mazda. For in the sixth epoch there will come about in a great number of people through contemplation of their own inner being, through a new recognition of the Sun Being who was revealed in ancient Persia, something like a recapitulation but of an infinitely more sublime, more spiritual and more intimate character.

I have already said that when the Greeks in their way and after their own fashion spoke of Ahura Mazda they called him Apollo. In their mysteries they allowed individuals to become acquainted with the deeper essence of this Apollo. Above all they saw in Apollo the spirit who not only directed the physical sun forces, but who also guided and directed the spiritual sun forces to the earth. And when the teachers in those Apollonian mysteries desired to speak to their pupils of the spiritual and moral influences of Apollo, they said that Apollo filled the entire earth with the holy music of the spheres, that is to say, he sent down rays from the spiritual world. And they saw in Apollo a being accompanied by the Muses, his assistants. A wonderful and deep wisdom is wrapped up in Apollo and his nine Muses. Man's being consists of physical body, etheric body, astral body, sentient soul, intellectual soul, consciousness soul and so on; man is an 'I'-centre, having seven or nine members around it, all of which are parts of its being. Let us ascend from a human being to a divine being, and think of the 'I' as this divine being, and of the members as his helpers, each helper being a single individuality. Even as in man the different members, physical body, etheric body, astral body and so on are gathered together and grouped around his 'I', so were the Muses grouped around Apollo. What was said in connection with this subject to those about to be initiated into the Apollonian mysteries is of a deep significance. A secret was confided to them, and the secret was this: that the god who in the second epoch had spoken such wonderful words to Zarathustra would speak to people in the sixth epoch in a very special way. This was the intention and meaning of the saying that in the sixth period the Song of Apollo upon earth would attain its goal. In this saying, which was frequently quoted by the pupils of the Apollonian mystery schools, was expressed the fact that during the sixth epoch the second period of the Earth evolution would be recapitulated on a higher stage. The first epoch will reappear in a higher form during the seventh period.

It is the highest possible ideal for present-day man to attain to the knowledge of the first post-Atlantean epoch as permeated by the Christ, to regain a way of feeling, of looking at things, which characterized the first post-Atlantean epoch, though then at a lower stage. Once again, at the conclusion of our post-Atlantean period, shall the individual who takes the path out into the external sense-world and who wrestles with what is revealed in his own soul-world, recognize that both these paths lead him to a unity. It is therefore good to transpose ourselves to some extent into that which for us today—for we are in the intermediate epoch—is the somewhat alien feeling and thinking of ancient Indian times. Even if we only find a few traces we nevertheless perceive something of the quite different character of feeling and thinking, of the quite different attitude to wisdom and life existing at that time when the 'I'-consciousness did not exist in human feeling in such an awakened form. What was written down in the Vedas was the teaching of the Holy Rishis, the great teachers of ancient India, and when we state that the Holy Rishis were inspired by the high individuality who guided the peoples of old Atlantis over into Asia, through what today is Europe, we are only recording a fact. In a certain way the

Holy Rishis were the pupils of this high individuality, of
Manu. And what did Manu communicate to them? Manu
communicated to them the way in which they had at that
time attained to the first post-Atlantean wisdom, knowledge
and cognition. For our modern methods of acquiring
knowledge, whether by observing external nature or by
descending into the inner life of the soul in the way that it has
become today, would have had no meaning at that time.

During the first period of civilization of the post-Atlantean
time among the old Indian people the etheric body was to a
far greater extent outside the physical body than is the case
today. The old Indian could make use of this etheric body
and of its organs if he gave himself up to it, if he did not go
out into the external life of the physical body and if, as it were,
he forgot that he was in a physical body. When he did this he
felt as if he were being lifted out of himself, like a sword out of
a scabbard. In this experience he became aware of something
which may be described as follows: 'I do not see with eyes or
hear with ears, or think with the physical organ of understanding; I make use of the organs of the etheric body.' And
this he did. Then, however, living wisdom rose before him—
not thoughts which people may think or have thought, but
thoughts according to which the gods without had fashioned
the world. Deeply immersed in spiritual life, the Indian knew
nothing about what we today call thought, fabricated as it is
by the instrument of the brain. He never thought things out
intellectually, or reasoned about them; he rose out of his
physical body into his etheric body, and from there he looked
all around him at the cosmic totality of the thought of the
gods, whence the world sprang forth. He saw in a flash the
gift proceeding from the divine world. With his etheric
organs he saw the thoughts of the gods depicted in the design
of all things. He had no need of logical thinking. Why must
we think logically? For the reason that we must find truth
through logical thinking, because we might otherwise make

mistakes in linking up chains of thought. If we were so organized that right thoughts coalesced of themselves, we should not require logic.

The old Indian did not require logic for he looked at the thoughts of the gods, which were right of themselves. He wove around himself an etheric, cosmic net, wove it out of the thoughts of the gods. He looked into this web of thought, which appeared to him like a soul-light pervading the world, and in it he saw the primordial, eternal wisdom. This highest stage of perfection, which I have just described to you, was of course only possible for the Holy Rishis, and with this vision they could proclaim great world realities. What kind of feeling did their visions arouse? They felt that into this world-web of wisdom, in which everything was written in living prototype, which was entirely woven of and irradiated by the soul of the light, truth and knowledge poured. Just as man of a later time feels something stream into him when he draws a breath, so the old Indian felt that the gods sent out wisdom to him and that he drew it in, even as the air is sent out to us in the breath that we draw in. Soul-light, and moreover soul-light pervaded by spiritual wisdom, it was that the ancient Holy Rishis drew in, and this they were able to teach to their disciples. They were justified in saying that everything which they proclaimed was breathed out by Brahman himself. That is the meaning of the deep expression, an expression which is verbally correct: 'It is breathed out by Brahman and breathed in by men.' That was the position of the Holy Rishis as regards the wisdom of the world, as regards the things which they made known. These were then written down in the different portions of the Vedas, in pictorial form, if the expression may be permitted; yet these forms were but feeble reproductions of the original visions.

We must always bear that truth in mind when reading the Vedas today, and not imagine that we are contemplating in its fullness the original sacred wisdom beheld by the ancient

Rishis. We must understand that the Vedas are of a different character to other writings.

Many documents of many kinds are to be found in the world. Speaking from our particular standpoint, for instance, we may say: 'We find an inward soul life pervaded and filled with the Christ in the Gospel of St John.' But if we consider the manner in which that Gospel is expressed, if we regard its exterior form, we find it less closely expressive of its contents than the medium used to embody the wisdom of the Vedas. There is a close connection between the outward expression and the inner content of the Vedas, because that which was breathed in was expressed in the Vedic words simultaneously, as it were; whereas the writer of St John's Gospel had its deep wisdom imparted to him at one time and wrote it down later; as a result the vision and the expression are further separated than in the Vedas.

We must understand these things clearly if we really wish to comprehend the evolution of the world. We must value the Gospel of St John more highly than anything else but it is also natural that a Christian should not be satisfied with the mere letter, but should penetrate through, as spiritual science does, into the spiritual content of the Gospel according to St John. It is natural that he should say: 'It only becomes what it ought to be to me when I pierce through into that of which it is the outer expression.' But anyone who wishes to adopt the right attitude towards the Vedas must feel as did the man of ancient India that what was to be found in the Vedas was not written down later by any man as the expression of divine wisdom. Therefore the Vedas, especially the Rig-Veda, are not only records of something holy, but are themselves sacred to those who perceive what they are. And hence arose the infinite veneration for the Vedas themselves in olden times, a reverence such as is offered to a divine being. That is the fact we must understand. And we must gain this understanding by contemplating the souls of the old Indian people. There are many things to be learned because we are advancing towards an ideal—the ideal of the first period of civilization at a higher stage, and of its re-establishment. We must learn to understand, for instance, what is said of Bharadvaja, that he studied the Vedas for three hundred years. A person of the present day would think he possessed mighty knowledge if he had studied the Vedas for three hundred years; he would think he knew a good deal even if he had studied them for a much shorter time. Yet it is related that one day the god Indra came to Bharadvaja and said to him: 'Thou hast now studied the Vedas for three hundred years; see, there are three very high mountains yonder. The first one represents the first part of the Vedas, the Rig-Veda; the second one represents the second part of the Vedas, the Sama-Veda; and the third one represents the third part of the Vedas, the Yagur-Veda. Thou hast studied these three parts of the Vedas for three hundred years.' Then Indra took three small lumps of earth out of these mountains, just so much as could be held in the hand, and said: 'Look at these lumps of earth; thy knowledge of the Vedas is as these lumps in proportion to yonder towering mountains.' If what is here said be transposed into a feeling, it is this: that if, in approaching the highest wisdom—whether it be in this or any other form, even in the form in which we find it today when we are called by the Rosicrucian method to seek for it not in books but by observation of what is to be found in the world—we can apply this story, we are taking the right attitude. Hardly anyone can say that he has heard as much about spiritual knowledge as had Bharadvaja about the Vedas; but everyone can make this comparison between himself and Bharadvaja, and he will then have put himself in the right relationship as far as his feelings are concerned with the all-embracing wisdom of the world. And he will be aware of something infinite of which we can only possess a small fraction. In this way, too, we get the right kind of yearning to go forward and to have patience until another little fraction of wisdom is added. Much may be learned from the ancient wisdom of the East; but among the most valuable things which can be learnt from the Light of the East are those which are connected with our feelings and our perceptions, and something of this can be learned in what the god Indra gave to Bharadvaja by way of instruction as to the right attitude to assume towards the Vedas.

Feelings of holy awe and reverence such as were felt in those ancient days must again be acquired by us if we would advance to an epoch wherein we may once more, through the disclosures made in the newer mysteries, penetrate into that veil of wisdom which is woven of divine and not of human thoughts. These feelings are the very highest we can acquire. But we must not think that we already possess them; we must clearly realize that knowledge alone leads up to these highest feelings. And if we avoid thinking, if we take life too easily and decline to seek the feelings that are to be found on the ethereal heights of thought, we shall experience only ordinary, trivial feelings and mistake them for what is obtained by the soul when it steeps itself in contemplation of divinity. Feelings such as were to be found among the old Indians were the essential means of approach to all the wisdom of the first post-Atlantean epoch, and to the ability to assume a right attitude towards the world in that age as well as to perceive that unity which is to be found in the spiritual worlds, whether upon the outward or the inward path. But in each successive civilization something new must come to light.

Whereas the old Indians realized that both paths led to the same goal, the old Persian, the Egypto-Chaldean and the Graeco-Roman epochs came to regard the two revelations from within and without as being in different directions. On the one hand we have the revelation coming from outside, and on the other the manifestation from within. This is already observable during the second epoch of the post-Atlantean civilizations. There we have on the one side not only the path of the people, but also the path of the mysteries, leading externally as well as inwardly to the realm of Ahura Mazda. That which was still a living reality in old Indian thought, the one-ness which was to be found in both the spiritual worlds, had already disappeared from the eyes of the second post-Atlantean civilization. That unity which had already withdrawn into impenetrable depths of existence could still be dimly sensed, but it could no longer live in the soul. The old Indian felt: 'Whether on the one side I go outwards or on the other side I go within, I come to the unity.' The Persian, in so far as he followed the teachings of Zarathustra, in following the outward path said: 'I come to Ormuzd,' or if he took the inward path, 'I come to the being of Mithras.' But in his consciousness these two paths were no longer united. At most he dimly sensed that they must be united somewhere. Therefore he spoke of that being who could then be sensed but dimly as the Unknown in Darkness, the unknown primeval god. This god, then, was a primeval spiritual being whose existence was not doubted, but whom people could no longer find. Zaruana Akarana was the name of this god existing in the darkness. That which could be reached lay behind the tapestry of the external sense world and Zarathustra's teaching laid special emphasis upon this phase. It was therefore something deriving from Zaruana Akarana, it was the god, Ahura Mazda, the lord in the realm of the sun spirits, in the realm from which the beneficent influences came down, which in contradistinction to the physical may be designated as the spiritual sun-influences. From this same spirit also did the old Persian civilization derive its moral precepts and laws, which the initiate—for it was he who by means of initiation raised himself to a knowledge of these precepts and laws—brought through as codes of morality and as laws for human conduct, for human functions, etc. That was one path, and people who followed it saw in the very highest region the Spirit of the Sun and his rule; they saw the servants of the Sun Spirit, the Amshaspands, arrayed as it were around his throne as his messengers. The Sun Spirit was lord over the whole realm; the Amshaspands directed the various activities. Beings of a lower order, subordinate in their turn to the Amshaspands, are generally called Izets or Izarads and finally beings of whom it may be said that they correspond in the spiritual world to the thoughts in the soul of man. Thoughts in the human soul are only the shadow reflections of realities; outside in the spiritual world they are spiritual beings. According to the old Persian conception these beings, called Fravashi (Feruers), were immediately above man. Thus during the old Persian evolution it was conceived that behind the covering of the sense world there were successive stages of spiritual beings rising higher and higher up to Ormuzd.

Now, the whole nature of old Persian humanity was different from that of the old Indian. The characteristic of an etheric body still to a great extent outside the physical body no longer obtained in the humanity of old Persia; the etheric body had by that time slipped very much further into the physical body. Therefore people of the old Persian civilization could no longer use the instruments of the etheric body in such a way as did the old Indians. The instruments used by the old Persians were the organs which originally formed part of what today we call the sentient or astral body.

The nine constituent parts of man, as we know, are as follows: Spirit Man, intellectual soul, Life Spirit, sentient soul, Spirit Self, astral body, consciousness soul, etheric body, and physical body.

As we have seen, the old Indian made use of his etheric body when he wished to raise himself up to realms of the highest knowledge. The Persian was no longer able to do this; but he could make use of his astral body, and this he did. Because he could no longer perceive through the etheric body, the highest unity was hidden from him but, by means of the astral body, to a certain extent he had still astral vision. This was the case with many members of the old, Persian people; astrally they saw Ahura Mazda and his servants because they were still able to make use of the astral body. Now you know from the description in my book *Theosophy* that the astral body is bound up with the sentient soul. When, therefore, a member of the old Persian nation made use of his astral body, his sentient soul also was present; but he could not make use of it because it was still undeveloped. He made use of his astral body in which the sentient soul was always a factor, but he had to take that soul just as it then was. Therefore he felt that when the astral body, developed as it then was, raised up to Ahura Mazda, the sentient soul was there also. The latter, however, was felt to be in some danger that, when revealing its perceptions, it would send them straight down into the astral body. The old Persian said to himself: 'The sentient soul will not externalize that which it encounters in the way of old luciferic temptations, but it will send their influences into the astral body.' He realized that influences from the sentient soul were working in upon the astral body, presenting, as it were, a reflection from the outer world of what had been at work in the sentient soul from ancient times. This is called the influence of Ahriman, of Mephistopheles.

And so man felt himself to be confronted by two powers. If he looked up to that which could be attained by directing his gaze outwards, he saw the mystery of Ahura Mazda; if he looked inwards he found himself, by the help of the astral body, but through the influence of Lucifer working in it, face to face with Ahriman, the opponent of Ahura Mazda. There was only one thing which could be any protection to him from the temptations of the ahrimanic beings, and that was to press onwards to initiation and the development of the sentient soul. By developing and purifying it and thus striding in advance of humanity, he took the path leading inwards that did not lead to Ahura Mazda, but to Lucifer's realms of light. And that which permeated the human soul upon the inward path was in later times called the god Mithras. Hence the Persian mysteries which cultivated the inner life were the mysteries of Mithras. On the one side therefore we have the god Mithras whom an individual met when he took the inward path and on the other the realms of Ahura Mazda, which he found on the outward path.

Now we will pass on to the next post-Atlantean civilization, to the Egypto-Chaldean period. There is good reason for giving it a double name. For on the one side we have throughout this epoch of civilization, over in Asia, people belonging to the northern stream of peoples who form the Chaldaic element; on the other side we have the Egyptian element, representing the stream of people who went more to the south. This is an epoch wherein two streams of nations encountered one another. And if we remember that the northern stream developed more particularly external vision, pursuing the reality of beings to be found behind the sense world, and that the Egyptian peoples sought for the spiritual beings to be found upon the inward path, we shall realize that two streams coexisted during this third epoch. The outward path taken by the Chaldeans and the inward path taken by the Egyptians came in contact. The Greeks were right when they compared the Chaldaic gods with their own Apollonian realms; they sought in their own way in their Apollonian mysteries for that which came to them from the Chaldeans. But when they spoke of Osiris and of that which was connected with him they sought for illumination through the mysteries of Dionysos. At that time people still had a consciousness of spiritual relationships. Now, in the course of its evolution mankind develops new members in the constitution of man. In the old Indian period the etheric body and its organs were developed; in the old Persian period people developed and used the astral body, and in the Egypto-

Chaldean period the sentient soul, that is to say, an inner member. Whereas the astral body is still directed outwards, the sentient soul is directed inwards. Hence man drew further away from the divine-spiritual worlds than was formerly the case. He lived an inner life in the soul and, as regards that which is not within him, life was limited to what the senses perceived. On the one side the world of sense grew more and more dominant, and on the other the soul life established its independence. The development of the sentient soul belonged to the third epoch. But what the sentient soul developed during the Egypto-Chaldean period was no longer wisdom that could be seen and read as it were from the external environment. It was a process resembling man's present thinking today, but it was much more alive, for the reason that man of today has already attained to the consciousness soul. Thoughts were then much richer, more full of life than is the case today. Man in these days does not experience his thoughts with the same intensity with which he becomes aware of a taste or a scent. During the Egyptian epoch, while the sentient soul was being intensively developed, thoughts were as vivid in the soul as is today the perception of colour, or scent, or taste. Today they have grown fainter and more abstract. In the Egyptian epoch they were concrete. They were more like visible thoughts; although not thoughts which could be said to take objective shape in the physical world they were nevertheless thoughts carrying with them a conviction that they had not been puzzled out, but rose in the soul like inspirations, surging in suddenly and presenting themselves in a flash. These people did not say that they breathed wisdom in, but that they were permeated by living thoughts, which sprang up out of the soul, which were impelled from the spiritual world into our own. Thus does everything change in the course of time.

And so a man belonging to the Egypto-Chaldean epoch no longer was conscious of the wisdom of the world spread out as a tapestry of light around him, to be breathed in. He was conscious of possessing thoughts which rose within him as inspirations. And the content of the science thus rising in man's being is Chaldaic astro-theology and Egyptian Hermetic wisdom. That which lives in the stars and moves them in their courses, that which pulsates in all things, could no longer be, as it were, read by man, but it revealed itself to his innermost being in the form of the ancient wisdom of the Egypto-Chaldean period. Moreover, old Chaldean people had the following feeling: 'That which I know is not only my inmost being; it is a reflection of what is taking place externally.' The old Egyptian felt what thus arises to be a reflection of the hidden gods whom people do not meet between birth and death, but between death and a new birth. Thus did the Egyptians and Chaldeans differ from each other, in that the latter realized through their wisdom what lies behind the world in which we live between birth and death, and the former, the Egyptians, realized through their inspired wisdom the living beings whom man encounters between death and a new birth. Necessarily, however, as may be seen from the whole purpose of this evolution, these inspirations from within, these massed thoughts arising as inspirations, were far removed from the conception of a primordial being in its unity. People could no longer penetrate as far as during the old Persian period when it was possible still to make use of the astral body. Impressions had all grown fainter; they were not so external, for the outer world had already withdrawn itself considerably. Accordingly people experienced wisdom of the external world within themselves, and no longer experienced the wisdom in the external world itself. Nevertheless those who had learned to appreciate the wisdom of the old Persian epoch in the right manner entertained for it feelings of high respect and deep gratitude. And if we need a short definition of the paradoxical wisdom with which the Chaldeans expressed that which they saw in the spiritual foundations underlying the physical world, we must call these utterances 'Chaldean Proverbs'; and the collection of Chaldean Proverbs was a very highly valued treasure of wisdom in the old times. World secrets of infinite importance are to be found therein. They were valued as highly as the revelations experienced between death and a new birth; and these were treasured as the source of Egyptian wisdom.

But that reality of which during the ancient Indian epoch there had been direct cognition became shadowy and dim; its deeper essence came to be entirely hidden from the eyes of man. This highest reality was still more shadowy to Egypto-Chaldean wisdom than Zaruana Akarana had been to the vision of old Persian seers. The Chaldeans called it Anu; Anu does in a sense express the unity of both worlds, but a unity far above man's knowledge. They did not venture to penetrate even into those regions into which the humanity of the time of Zarathustra looked up, but they turned their visions to spheres which were very near to human thought. Everything, they said, was to be found there, for the highest is to be found even in the lowest. But they also found something there expressive of the reality of a being, a shadowy reflection of the highest. This they named Apason. Apason seemed to them to be as a shadowy reflection of what we today conceive of as substance below Spirit Man, substance, as it were, formed out of Life Spirit. To this they gave a name whose nearest equivalent in English sound would be something like Tau-te. There was also a reality to which they gave the name of Moymis. Moymis was approximately that which spiritual science would describe as a world-spirit, a being whose lowest principle is the Spirit Self. Thus the old Chaldeans contemplated a trinity above them, but they were conscious of the fact that this trinity only manifested its real nature so far as its lower members were concerned, and that its higher members were only shadowy reflections of the highest, which had entirely withdrawn from them. And Bel, the god who as creator of the universe was also the national god, must be thought of as a descendant of this Moymis who had entered the region of egohood or of fire essence.

Thus we see how the essential nature of an entire people expressed itself even in the naming of the gods. When a person belonging to the old Chaldaic epoch took the path to his inner being, he spoke of having passed through the veil of soul life into a world of subhuman or subterranean gods. Adonis is a later name for the beings found by taking the inward path. This path was accessible to initiates only, for it was beset with great dangers for a non-initiate. And when an initiate trod this path, attaining on the one side to the world beyond the senses and on the other to the world that underlies the veil of the soul world, he experienced something comparable to the experiences encountered in initiation at the present day. Anyone initiated in ancient Chaldea went through two separate experiences, and care was taken to have them take place as nearly as possible at the same time. One experience was that of entering the spiritual world from the outer world, the other was being admitted into it from the inner world. And these two had to coincide as far as possible in order that the candidate might learn to feel that the same spiritual forces were expressing themselves through spiritual life and interaction both without and within. On the inward way he met the spiritual being called Ishtar, who was known to be a beneficent moon divinity, and who stood on the threshold that hides from man the spiritual element standing behind his soul life. On the other side, where the door opening through the outer sense world into the world of spirit is situated, stood the Guardian Merodach or Mardach, and he stood there with Ishtar. Merodach (whom we may compare with the Guardian of the Threshold, with Michael) and Ishtar were the pair who imparted clairvoyance to the soul and led people by both paths into the spiritual world. That experience is still expressed symbolically today by the saying that 'the shining cup is given to man to drink from'. That is, as if by a draught he learns to experience the very first activities of his lotus flowers. Thereafter he made further progress. What we must bear in mind is that it was necessary to step across a certain threshold even at that time.

In Egypt the procedure was not identical though similar. Then came the epoch which was to prepare for the descent of the cosmic Sun God upon the earth. The spirit who previously had been external now had to enter into the human soul, had to be found within it, even as formerly the luciferic divinities and Osiris were to be found there. The two paths clearly shown in the contrasts between the Chaldeans and the Egyptians had to make each other fruitful. Such an event was essential. How could it take place? It could only occur after a 'connecting link' had been created. This proceeded from Ur of Chaldea, as the Bible truly states. It takes up the revelation coming from without, then it passes on into Egypt, absorbs that which comes from within and unites the two, so that for the first time in Yahweh we have a being heralding the Christ who unites the two paths. Yahweh or Jehovah is a divinity to be found on the inward path, but in himself Yahweh is not visible. He only becomes visible when illuminated from without. Jehovah reflects the light of Christ. Here we can clearly see the two paths we have been studying so intensely running side by side and each fructifying the other. And when this begins, quite a new process becomes apparent in human evolution. The outward and the inward fructify each other; the inward becomes the external and that which formerly lived only inwardly and within time now spreads out into space, so that the two paths continue side by side. Consider your own soul life! It does not spread out in 'space', it runs its course in 'time'. Thoughts and feelings follow one another—in 'time'. That which is outside is spread out in space, in simultaneous coexistence. Accordingly an event had to happen which may be called the 'outflow into space and coexistence' of something which till then had only lived in time. And that event duly took place; something which had hitherto lived only in time became from that epoch onward a coexisting life in space. In this manner occurred a change of profound importance and one to which expression was given in an equally profound manner.

All previous human spiritual evolution in leading out beyond the external world of space led also into external time. Now, everything that comes under the laws of time is regulated by the measure and the nature of the number seven. We learn to understand the evolution of the world by basing it upon the number seven and counting, for example, the seven stages of Old Saturn, Old Sun, Old Moon, Earth (or Mars-Mercury), Jupiter, Venus and Vulcan. In everything which has to do with time we proceed aright by making use of the number seven. In 'time' we are everywhere led to the number seven. All the schools and lodges whose teachings lead out of space into time have seven as a fundamental number when they lead to the supersensible. This number seven is associated with the Holy Rishis, and with the holy teachers of other nations down to the seven wise men of Greece. But the fundamental number of space is twelve, and in flowing into space time is revealed according to the number twelve. At the point where time flows out into space the number twelve dominates. We have twelve tribes in Israel, also twelve Apostles at the moment when Christ, who had previously revealed Himself in time, poured out into space. What is within time occurs in succession. Hence that which leads out of space into time, to gods of the luciferic realms, leads into the number seven. If we would characterize anything in this realm according to its essence, we find the being by going back to the ancestry. In order to perceive that which develops itself in time we pass from the later back to the earlier, as from child to father. On going into the world of time, in which the number seven obtains, we speak of children and of their origin, of the children of spiritual beings, of the children of Lucifer; when we lead time out into space we speak of beings existing simultaneously, in whose nature, coexistence and also the flowing of souls, the impulses from one to another in space demand our consideration.

Where the number seven, through the fact that time pours out into space, changes into twelve, the connotation of 'children' ceases to have the same supersensible meaning and the connotation of 'brotherhood' enters, for beings who live side by side are brothers. The concept of sons of gods is changed in the course of evolution into the concept of brothers living side by side.

Brothers and sisters live side by side. Beings who descend from one another live after one another. Here we see the transition, at a significant epoch, from the sons or children of Lucifer's kingdom and of his being to the brothers of Christ, a transition of which we shall speak further.

LECTURE 9

The Bodhisattvas and the Christ

31 August 1909

The facts stated at the end of the last lecture cannot but be
somewhat unintelligible to persons who encounter them for
the first time, for they belong to the secrets of numbers. And
the secrets of numbers are those which are in a comparative
sense the most difficult to master.

It has been stated that there is a certain relation between
the numbers seven and twelve, and that this relation has
something to do with time and space. Now this profound
mystery can, gradually, be understood by everybody, but it
must necessarily remain a mere statement to the kind of
cognition which today is alone recognized as such. It has to
be elucidated, explained. An understanding of the 'mach-
inery' of the world may be reached, as I have already indicated, by distinguishing between conditions which are
essentially those of space and conditions which belong
essentially to time. We understand the world which surrounds us primarily in terms of space and time; but if we do
not confine ourselves to speaking of time and space in an
abstract sense and endeavour to understand how conditions
are regulated in time and how the different beings in space
are related to each other, we find a thread leading on the one
side through the complicated relations of time, and on the
other through the complex conditions of space. In the first
place we observe the course of world events in the light of
spiritual science. We look back at earlier incarnations of man,
of races and civilizations, as well as of the Earth itself. We
build up within ourselves an idea of what will happen in the

future, i.e. in time. And we shall always see our way if we judge of evolution in time from a framework built up by means of the number seven.

We must not build and speculate and attribute all kinds of meanings to the number seven; we must only pursue the facts from the point of view of the number seven. In the first place this number seven is only a means of facilitating our task. Take, for instance, an individual whose spiritual vision is so far opened that he can examine data of the Akashic Records of the past. He may use the number seven as a guide and realize that what runs its course in time is built up on the basis of the number seven; that which repeats itself in various forms can very well be analysed by using the number seven as a foundation and proceeding from this as a basis. In this sense it is right to say that since the Earth goes through various embodiments we have to look for its seven incarnations: Old Saturn, Old Sun, Old Moon, Earth, Jupiter, Venus and Vulcan. Because human civilizations pass through seven incarnations we must seek their connections by once more using the number seven as a basis. Let us for instance consider the civilizations in post-Atlantean times. The old Indian is the first, the second is the old Persian, the third the Egypto-Chaldean, the fourth the Graeco-Roman, the fifth our own and we are expecting two more, the sixth and seventh, to succeed our own. We can also find our way in the study of the karma of an individual by trying to look at his three former incarnations. By starting with the incarnation of a person of the present day and looking back at his three former incarnations it is possible to draw certain conclusions concerning his next three incarnations. The three former and the present incarnations plus the three following make seven again. Seven is a clue for everything that happens in time.

On the other hand the number twelve is a clue for all things that coexist in space. Science, which at the same time was wisdom, was always conscious of this. It said: 'It is possible to find the right way by connecting the spatial relationship of everything that occurs upon earth with twelve permanent points in space—the twelve signs of the zodiac in the cosmos.' These are the twelve basic points with which everything in space is connected. This declaration was not an arbitrary yield of human thinking. But the power of thought in those early times had learned from reality and so ascertained the fact that space was best understood when it was divided into twelve constituent parts, thus making the number twelve a clue for all spatial relations. However, where the question of changes came in, that is to say in the time element, the seven planets were given as a clue by a still older science. Seven is here the clue.

Now how does this apply to the evolution of human life? We have said that up to the point of time in human evolution characterized by the advent of the Christ impulse it is a fact that when a man looked into his inner being, when he sought the way to the world of the gods through the veil of his inner being, he entered the luciferic world—to use a collective name. This too was the path upon which, in those olden times, man sought for wisdom, upon which he sought to acquire a higher knowledge concerning the world than he could find behind the covering of the external sense world. His quest consisted in sinking down into his inner world; for in this world the intuitions and inspirations of moral and ethical life originated, just as the intuitions of conscience arose there. And of course all other intuitions and inspirations which pertain to the moral nature, to that which belongs to the soul, arose out of that soul world. Hence those lofty individualities who were the leaders of mankind in ancient times had of necessity first to contact the inner life of an individual if they wanted to give instruction upon that which belongs to the highest in humanity. The Holy Rishis had to contact the soul life of man, his inner being, that is, as did all the great teachers of humanity in older civilizations. But the soul life of man belongs to time; it runs its course in time. That which surrounds us externally groups itself in space; that which runs its course inwardly groups itself in time. Hence everything which is to speak to the inner being of man must use the clue of the number seven. How can we best understand a being with a message for the inner life of man? How, for instance, can we best understand those beings with their fundamentally individual characteristics whom we call the Holy Rishis? By relating them to soul life which runs its course in time. Hence in those ancient epochs wherein the great sages spoke, one question above all was asked: 'Whence have they descended?' Just as we might ask a son 'Who are your father and mother?' so ancestry, the time element, was then the subject of enquiry. On meeting a wise man the primary concern was: Whence does he come? Who was the being who preceded him? What is his descent? Whose son is he? Therefore in speaking about the luciferic world, the number seven had to be taken as basic and the interest was whose child it was who was speaking to the human soul. We speak of the children of Lucifer in this sense when we speak of those who in olden times taught of the spiritual world lying hidden behind the veil of soul life, behind that which belongs to time.

But the Christ comes under a different category altogether. The Christ did not descend to earth by the path of time. The Christ came to earth at a certain point of time, but from outside, from space. Zarathustra saw Him when he directed his gaze to the sun, and spoke of Him as Ahura Mazda. To the spiritual vision of man in space Ahura Mazda came nearer and nearer until He descended and became Man. Here therefore the interest lies in the approach through space, not in the time sequence. The approach through space, this advent of the Christ out of the infinitude of space down to our earth, has an eternal and not a temporal value. With this is connected the fact that Christ's work upon earth is not carried on only under the conditions of time. He does not bring to earth anything corresponding to the relationships between father and child, or mother and child, which exist under time conditions, but He brings into the world something which goes on side by side, which coexists. Brothers live side by side, they coexist. Parents, children and grandchildren live after one another in time, and the conditions of time express their individual relation to each other. But the Christ as the Spirit of Space brings a spatial element into the civilization of the earth. What Christ brings is the coexistence of human beings in space, a condition of increasing community of soul regardless of time conditions. The mission of the earth planet in our cosmic system is to bring love into the world. In olden days the task of earth was to bring in love with the help of time. Inasmuch as through the conditions of ancestry and descent the blood poured itself from generation to generation, from father to child and grandchildren, those who were connected through time were *ipso facto* those who loved each other. Family connections, blood relationships, the descending stream of blood through the generations, following each other in time, provided the foundation of love in the olden times. And the cases where love took on more of a moral character were also rooted in the conditions of time. People loved their ancestors, those who had preceded them in time. Through Christ there came the love of soul to soul, so that that which is side by side, which coexists in space, enters a relationship which was at first represented by brothers and sisters living side by side and—at the same time—the relationship of brother love which one human soul is intended to bear towards another in space. Here the condition of coexistent life in space begins to acquire its special significance.

Hence in the olden times, it was natural to speak of those who were connected by the rule of the number seven: the Seven Rishis, and the Seven Sages. But Christ is surrounded by twelve Apostles in whom we see the prototypes of man living side by side, coexisting in space. And this love which, independently of successive ages, is to encompass all that exists side by side in space, will enter social life on earth through the Christ principle. To love what is around us with brother love, that is to follow Christ. If, therefore, we speak in the olden times of the children of Lucifer, the Christ principle is the impulse which causes us to say: 'Christ is the firstborn of many brethren.' And the brotherhood relationship to Christ—feeling oneself drawn not as to a father but as to a brother whom one loves as an elder brother, but nevertheless as a brother—is the fundamental relationship which people have learned to assume in consequence of the descent of the Christ principle upon the earth.

These of course are only instances which illustrate and make clear, although they do not prove, the relation between the numbers seven and twelve. The more, therefore, that the Christ influence shines down into the world, the more allusion is made to the nature and reality of things by grouping them in twelves—as, for instance, the twelve tribes of Israel, the twelve Apostles, and so on. In this connection the number twelve has a mystical and secret meaning as regards the evolution of the Earth.

This may be termed the external aspect, the outer view of the great change which took place in Earth evolution through the infusion of the Christ principle. We might speak at great length about the relation of the number seven to the number twelve and have to leave much that concerns the deep mysteries of our universe still incomprehensible. If what has been said in elucidation of the numbers seven and twelve be taken as clues to the relationships existing in time and in space, we shall be able to penetrate more and more deeply into the secrets of the universe. But for all of us this relation between the numbers seven and twelve should, in the first place, be one which apart from everything else indicates how profoundly momentous the Christ event was for the world, and how necessary it is thenceforth to seek another numerical clue if we are to find our way in it.

But there is also an inner relationship of space and time with which the numbers twelve and seven have something to do which I can only indicate here in bare outline. And my illustration shall be made as was usual in the mysteries when the relation of twelve to seven in the cosmos was being portrayed. It has been said that if we do not consider universal space in an abstract sense, but really relate earth conditions to universal space, we must refer those earth conditions to the circle described by the twelve essential points of the zodiac, namely Aries, Taurus, Gemini, Cancer, Leo, Virgo, Libra, Scorpio, Sagittarius, Capricorn, Aquarius, Pisces. These twelve points of the zodiac were not alone the real and veritable world symbols for the very oldest divine spiritual beings, but the symbols themselves were thought to correspond, in a certain sense, with reality. Even when the Earth was embodied as Old Saturn, the forces issuing from these twelve directions were at work upon that ancient planet; likewise, later they were also on the Old Sun, and on the Old Moon, and are now and will continue to be in the future. They have, therefore, the nature of permanence, as it were; they are far more sublime than that which arises and passes away within our earth existence. That which is symbolized by the twelve signs of the zodiac is infinitely higher than that which is transformed in the evolutionary course of our planet from Old Saturn to Old Sun and from that to Old Moon and so on. Planetary existence arises and passes away, but the zodiac is ever there. What is symbolized by the points of the zodiac is more sublime than what upon our earth plays its part as the opposition between good and evil.

In an earlier lecture I called your attention to the fact that on penetrating into the astral realm we enter a world of change—where something which from one point of view works for good may from another point of view appear as evil. On the one hand, these differences between good and evil have their meaning in evolution and seven is the key number; on the other hand, that which is the symbol of the gods in the twelve points in space, in the twelve points of permanence, is above good and evil. Out in space we have to seek for the symbols of those divine-spiritual beings which considered in themselves and without reference to their effects upon our earthly sphere are beyond the differences between good and evil.

But now let us conceive that which becomes our earth beginning to be active. That can only happen by a division, as it were, coming to pass in the permanent gods, and that which takes place entering into a different relation to these gods of permanence, who are divided into two spheres, a sphere of good and a sphere of evil. In themselves neither is good nor evil; but inasmuch as it influences the evolution of Earth it is sometimes good, sometimes evil. So that all that belongs to the one may be described as the sphere of goodness, and that which belongs to the other as the sphere of evil.

In order to obtain the correct conception, we must consider the civilizations of the post-Atlantean era, which had gone through the old Indian, the old Persian, the Egypto-Chaldean civilizations, and which will also go through the civilizations which are to follow these, up to the next great catastrophe, and beyond it. If we enquire where there is a truer image of what runs through the whole evolution of mankind than can be found using sense-perception or the human intellect, we must turn to occult science and ask what is to be discovered in the spiritual world which moves more or less as a continuous spiritual stream through all these seven civilizations. In the wisdom of the East a word has been formed for that which runs through all these civilizations; it is (if one considers its real nature) not an abstraction, but something concrete—it is a Being. And if we wish to describe this Being more intimately—this Being of whom in reality all other beings, whether the seven Holy Rishis or even higher beings who do not descend into physical incarnation are the messengers—we may designate it by a name which has rightly been used by the East. Every revelation and all the wisdom in the world can be traced back finally to this one source, the source of primeval wisdom, under the dominion of a Being who evolves onwards through each and all of the above-named civilizations of the post-Atlantean era, who appears in each epoch in one form or another, but who is always One Being, the bearer of wisdom which has appeared in the most varied guise. When I described in the last lecture how the Holy Rishis breathed in this wisdom and took it in concretely, this soul of the light which was spread abroad externally and was breathed in as light-wisdom by the Holy Rishis, was the out-flowing of that sublime Being (I cannot go into this fully here)—we must understand that what only belongs in minor degree to the sphere of goodness must also be called good. As soon as that which in the spiritual world—which as I have said is permanent, eternal, having nothing to do with time—passes into time, it divides itself into good and evil. Of the twelve points of permanence there remain belonging to the good the five actually within the sphere of good and two on the border, making seven. Therefore we speak of seven as remaining over from the twelve. When we wish to speak of that which is good and which acts as our guide in time, we must speak of Seven Sages, of Seven Rishis, for this corresponds to reality. Hence also comes the conception that seven signs of the zodiac belong to the world of light, to the upper world, and that the lower five beginning with Scorpio belong to the world of darkness.

This is only a mere indication serving to show that space, when it forsakes its sphere of eternity and takes into itself created things which run their course in time, is divided into good and evil; and in bringing out the good, seven is raised out of the twelve; seven then becomes the true number for temporal conditions. For truths, which belong to time, we must take the number seven as our clue; the remainder, the number five would lead us into error. That is the inner meaning of these things.

Do not at the moment imagine that this is very difficult to understand, but realize rather that the world is very profound and that there must be things whose meaning is very hard to fathom.

Christ came into the world to sit down even with publicans and sinners. He came in order to take up that which would otherwise have had to be cast out of the world process. In the story of Oedipus the same thing had to be cast out that in the Christ-life was gathered up as a leaven, as was corroborated by the story of Judas. Just as new bread must be leavened with a small portion of the old if it is to rise and spread, so the new world must take in a leaven made of something which came out of evil. Hence, Judas, who had been cast out from every place, who had even made himself impossible at the court of Pilate, could be admitted where the Christ was working—He who came to heal the world in such a way that the seven could be changed into the twelve and that which had been represented by the number seven might henceforth be represented by the number twelve. The number twelve is in the first instance represented to us by the twelve brothers of Christ, by the twelve disciples.

This must serve merely as a hint of the profound change that thus came into our whole Earth evolution. It is possible to elucidate the significance of the Christ principle, and of its entrance into the evolution of the Earth, from many different points of view, and what has just been touched upon is one of them.

Now let us once more place before our souls that which is a consequence of all that has gone before. It is felt and recognized by spiritual science, wherever it is truly cultivated, that with Christ something very special entered into the evolution of the Earth. Wherever true spiritual science is studied, it is felt and recognized that there is one thing which runs through all the beings of whom we are now speaking. And what we then described as their wisdom had poured down in other ages (for instance, in that quite different conception which was expressed in the old Persian epoch) from the same one being who is the Great Teacher of all civilizations. The being who was the teacher of the Holy Rishis, of Zarathustra, of Hermes—the being whom we may designate as the Great Teacher, who in the different ages manifests Himself in the most various ways, the being who as is natural at first remains entirely concealed from external vision—is designated, by means of an expression borrowed from the East, as the totality of the Bodhisattvas. The Christian conception would designate it the Holy Spirit. The Bodhisattva is a being who passes through all civilizations, who can manifest Himself to mankind in various ways. Such is the Spirit of the Bodhisattvas. All the ages have looked up to the Bodhisattvas. The Holy Rishis, Zarathustra, Hermes and Moses looked up to them—it matters not how they named the Being in whom they perceived the embodiment of the Bodhisattva principle. The Bodhisattva can be given this one name, 'The Great Teacher', and to him those individuals looked who wished to receive and could receive the teachings of the post-Atlantean era. This Bodhisattva spirit of the post-Atlantean era has taken human form many times, but one such interests us in particular. A Bodhisattva took on that radiant human form of the being of Gautama Buddha—it does not for the moment concern us in what other fashion he was also manifest. And it signified an advance of this Bodhisattva when it was no longer necessary for him to remain in the upper spiritual realms, when his development in the spiritual worlds was such that he could master his physical corporeality to the extent of becoming man as the Buddha. A Bodhisattva advancing in human existence is the Buddha. The Buddha is one of the human incarnations of the all-embracing wisdom figures underlying the evolution of the earth. In the Buddha we have the incarnation of that Great Teacher who may be called the essence of wisdom itself. The Buddha is the Bodhisattva who has become an earth being. And it is unnecessary to believe that a Bodhisattva incarnated in only the Buddha; for one of the Bodhisattvas has incarnated either wholly or in part in other human personalities. Such incarnations are not all similar; it must be quite clear that just as a Bodhisattva lived in the etheric body of Gautama Buddha, so likewise one also lived in the members of other human individuals. And because the being of that Bodhisattva who inherited the astral body of Zarathustra streamed into the members of other individualities, for instance Hermes, we may—but only if we understand the matter in this sense—call other individualities who also are great teachers an incarnation of a Bodhisattva. It is permissible to speak of ever-recurring incarnations of the Bodhisattva, but we must understand that behind all the men in whom the incarnation took place the Bodhisattva stood as a part of that being who is the personified All-Wisdom of our world.

In this sense, then, we gaze upon the wisdom-element which in olden times was imparted to mankind from the luciferic worlds. When we gaze upon this we are looking at the Bodhisattvas. Now, in post-Atlantean evolution there is a Being who is fundamentally different from a Bodhisattva and not to be confused with the latter, although this Being of whom we are here speaking was once incarnate in a human individuality who at the same time received the in-pouring of the Bodhisattva-Buddha being. Because a man once lived in whom the Christ incarnated and because at the same time the radiations of the Bodhisattva entered this human individuality, we must not take the essential thing in this incarnation to be the embodiment of the Bodhisattva in the personality who was Jesus of Nazareth. During the last three years the Christ principle was predominant and the Christ principle and the Bodhisattva principle are fundamentally different. How can we instance this difference? It is exceedingly important for us to know whereby the Christ, who was once incarnate in a human body—only once, never before and never after—could so incarnate. Since that time He can be reached by the path which leads to the inner essence of the human soul; before that time He was accessible if the gaze, as was the case with Zarathustra, was directed outwards.

Wherein, then, does the difference consist between the Christ, between that being to whom we must ascribe such a central position, and a Bodhisattva? It consists in this, that the Bodhisattva is the Great Teacher, the incarnation of wisdom, which pervades all the civilizations, which incarnates in many different ways; but the Christ is not only a teacher—that is the essential point. Christ is not only a teacher of mankind. He is a Being whom we can best understand if we expand to the sphere where in dazzling spiritual heights we can find Him as an object of Initiation and where we may compare Him with other spiritual beings. There are regions of spiritual life where, freed of all the dust of earth, we may find the sublime Bodhisattva Being in his spiritual essence and where we may find the Christ stripped of all that He became on earth or in its vicinity. There we find the origin of humanity, the source whence all life proceeds: the primeval, spiritual source. We find not only one Bodhisattva but a series of Bodhisattvas.

Even as there is a Bodhisattva who underlies our seven successive civilizations, so there was a Bodhisattva underlying the Atlantean civilizations, and so on. We find in these spiritual heights a series of Bodhisattvas who were, for their age, the great teachers and instructors not only of mankind but also of those beings who do not descend into the region of physical life. We find them there as the great teachers; there they gather that which they are to teach, and in their midst is One Being who is great not only because He teaches, and that is the Christ. He is not alone great because He teaches, rather is He a being who works upon the Bodhisattvas who surround Him, by manifesting Himself to them. He is seen by the Bodhisattvas and He reveals His glory to them. The Bodhisattvas are what they are through being great teachers; the Christ is to the world what He is through His own Being, through His own Essence. He needs only to be seen, and the manifestation of His own Being needs only to be reflected in His surroundings for the teachings to spring forth. He is not only a teacher; He is Life, a Life that pours itself into the other beings, who then become teachers.

The Bodhisattvas are mighty teachers because from their spiritual heights they enjoy the bliss of being able to see Christ. And when in the course of the evolution of our Earth we find incarnations of the Bodhisattvas we speak of great teachers of mankind, because the Bodhisattva principle is the most essential in them. The Christ does not only teach; we learn of Christ in order to understand Him, in order to recognize what He is. Christ is more an object than a subject of learning. The difference between Christ and the Bodhisattvas is that He is to the world what He is, because the world is blessed by sight of Him. The Bodhisattvas are to the world what they are because they are great teachers. Therefore if we wish to look up to the living being, to the life-source of our earth, we must look at the incarnation in which was embodied not a Bodhisattva—in which this fact was the most important feature of the incarnation—but a being who did not Himself leave any teaching behind, but who gathered round Him those who spread Gospels and teachings concerning Him over the whole world.

The point of prime importance is that no document exists

written by Christ Himself, but that teachers surround Him and speak about Him, so that He is the object and not the subject of the teaching. It is a remarkable circumstance and one of utmost importance with reference to the Christ event that nothing has been received from Him Himself, but that others have written about His being. It is therefore not to be wondered at that we are told we can find all the teachings of Christ in other faiths also; for Christ is in nowise merely a teacher. He is a Being who desires to be understood as a Being; He does not wish to sink into us only through His teachings, but through His life. We may gather together all the teachings in the world that are accessible to us, and we shall even then not have sufficient to enable us to understand the Christ. If people of the present day cannot turn directly to the Bodhisattvas and, with the spiritual eyes of the Bodhisattvas, look up to Christ, then they must learn from these Bodhisattvas what can eventually make Christ comprehensible. If therefore we wish not only to become participant in Christ but to understand Him, we must not only look at what Christ has done for us but we must learn of all the teachers of West and of East, and we must account it a holy thing to become familiar with the teachings of the whole known world. We must devote ourselves to the sacred task of understanding the Christ in His completeness by means of the highest teaching.

Now the mysteries always make appropriate preparation for the corresponding duty of mankind. Every age has its special task; and every age has to receive the truth in the particular form needed by that epoch. Truth in its present form could not have been given to the old Indian or to the old Persian. The truth had to be given to them in the form suitable to their capacities of perception. Therefore in the age which owing to its other characteristics was best suited to receive the Christ upon earth—that is to say, the fourth or Graeco-Roman epoch—the truth about Christ and about the world connected with Him was brought to mankind in a form adapted for humanity of that time. To believe that in the age following directly on the Christ-manifestation the whole truth about the Christ was already known is to be in complete ignorance concerning the progress of the human race. He who believes only the teaching of the first centuries after the Christ event, who considers what was written and recorded then to be the only true Christian teaching, knows nothing of human progress; he does not know that the greatest teacher of the first Christian centuries could tell him no more about Christ than the people of that time were able to assimilate. And because the people of the first Christian centuries were pre-eminently such as had descended the most deeply into the physical world, their understanding permitted them to take in comparatively little of the highest teaching concerning Christ. The majority of the early Christians could understand but little about the Christ Being.

We know that in old Indian times men possessed a high degree of clairvoyance in consequence of the relation of the etheric body to the other members; but the time had not then come for this vision to perceive the Christ as anything other than Vishvakarman—a spirit in distant regions beyond the sense world. In the time of the old Persian civilization it was first possible dimly to sense the Christ behind the physical sun. And so it went on. It was possible for Moses to perceive the Christ, as Jehovah, in thunder and lightning that is quite near the earth. And in the person of Jesus of Nazareth the Christ was seen incarnated as man. This is the manner of human progress; in old India wisdom was absorbed through the etheric body, in the old Persian period through the astral body, in the Egypto-Chaldean period through the sentient soul, in the Graeco-Roman period through that which we call the intellectual soul. The intellectual soul is bound to the world of sense. Therefore it lost the vision of what extends far, far beyond the sense world. Accordingly in the first

Christian centuries little more of existence was seen than that which lies between birth and death, and that which directly follows as the nearest spiritual region. Nothing was known of that which passes through many incarnations. This was due to the condition of human understanding. Only one part of the life cycle could be made intelligible, man's life on earth, and the fragment of spiritual life which follows it. That, therefore, is what we find described for the mass of the people. But that was not to continue. The outlook of man had to be prepared for an excursion beyond this part of his understanding. Preparation had to be made for a gradual revival of the all-embracing wisdom which man was able to enjoy in the time of Hermes, of Moses, of Zarathustra and of the old Rishis, as well as for offering us the possibility of an ever-increasing understanding of Christ. Christ had to come into the world just at a time when the means of under-standing were most contracted. The way had to be opened for the revival of the ancient wisdom during the ages to come and for placing it gradually in the service of the under-standing of Christ. This could only be accomplished by the creation of mystery wisdom.

Those people who came over into and beyond Europe from old Atlantis brought with them great wisdom. In old Atlantis the majority of the people were instinctively clair-voyant; they could see into spiritual realms. This clairvoy-ance could not develop further, and withdrew perforce into separate personalities in the West. It was guided there by a being who once upon a time lived in deepest concealment, withdrawn behind those who had already forsaken the world and who were pupils of the great initiates. This being had remained behind in order to preserve for later ages what was brought over from old Atlantis. Among the great initiates who had founded mystery places in the West for the pre-servation of the old Atlantean wisdom, a wisdom that entered deeply into all the secrets of the physical body, was the great

Skythianos, as he was called in the Middle Ages. And anyone who knows the nature of the European mysteries knows that Skythianos is the name given to one of the greatest initiates of the earth.

But there also lived in the world for a long, long time the being which in a spiritual sense we may describe as the Bodhisattva. This Bodhisattva was the same being who after completing its task in the West was incarnated in Gautama Buddha about six hundred years before our era. This exalted being who, as Teacher, had by that time withdrawn more towards the East was a second great Teacher, a second great Keeper of the Seal of the wisdom of mankind. There was also a third individuality destined to greatness of whom we have spoken in various lectures. It is he who was the teacher of the old Persians, the great Zarathustra. The three great spiritual beings and individualities known to us under the names of Zarathustra, Gautama Buddha and Skythianos are, as it were, incarnations of Bodhisattvas. That which lived in them was not the Christ.

Mankind had now to be given time to experience in itself the advent of Christ who had formerly made Himself manifest to Moses upon Mount Sinai; Jehovah was the same Being as Christ, though wearing another form. Time had to be allowed to mankind in which to prepare to receive the Christ. That occurred in the epoch in which the comprehension for such things reached the nadir. But preparation had to be made, in order that understanding and wisdom should again grow greater and greater; and this was part of Christ's mission on earth.

There is a fourth individuality named in history behind whom for those who have the proper comprehension much lies hidden—an individuality still higher and more powerful than Skythianos, than the Buddha or than Zarathustra. This individuality is Manes, and those who see more in Manichaeism than is usually the case know him to be a very high messenger of Christ. It is said that a few centuries after Christ had lived on earth there was held one of the greatest assemblies of the spiritual world connected with earth that ever took place, and that there Manes gathered round him three mighty personalities of the fourth century after Christ. In this figurative description a most significant fact in connection with spiritual development is expressed. Manes called these persons together to consult with them as to the means of reintroducing the wisdom that had lived throughout the changing times of the post-Atlantean age and of causing it to unfold more and more gloriously in the future. Who were the personalities brought together by Manes in that memorable assembly? It should be remembered that such an event can only be witnessed by spiritual sight. Manes called together the personality in whom Skythianos lived at that time, and also the physical reflection of the Buddha who had then appeared again, and the erstwhile Zarathustra who was wearing a physical body at that time. Around Manes was this council, himself in the centre and around him Skythianos, the Buddha and Zarathustra. And in that council a plan was agreed upon for causing all the wisdom of the Bodhisattvas of the post-Atlantean time to flow more and more strongly into the future of mankind; and the plan of the future evolution of the civilizations of earth then decided upon was adhered to and carried over into the European mysteries of the Rosy Cross. These particular mysteries have always been connected with the individualities of Skythianos, of the Buddha and of Zarathustra. They were the teachers in the schools of the Rosy Cross—teachers who gave their wisdom to earth as a gift, in order that through it the Christ Being might be understood. Hence in all spiritual Rosicrucian schools the deepest reverence is paid to these old initiates who preserved the primeval wisdom of Atlantis: to the reincarnated Skythianos, in whom was seen the great and honoured Bodhisattva of the West; to the temporarily incarnated reflection of the Buddha, who also was honoured as one of the Bodhisattvas; and finally to Zarathustra, the reincarnated Zarathustra. These were looked up to as the great Teachers of the European initiates. Such presentations must not be taken in the sense of external history, although they elucidate the historical course of events better than any external description could do.

Let me illustrate this statement by saying that there is hardly to be found a single country in the Middle Ages in which a certain legend was not everywhere current, though at that time no one in Europe knew anything of Gautama Buddha, and the tradition of Gautama Buddha had been completely lost. Yet the following story was related (it is to be found in many books of the Middle Ages and is one of the widely disseminated stories of that period). Once upon a time there was a king in India to whom a son was born called Josaphat. Extraordinary things were prophesied about this child when he was born. His father therefore especially guarded him; he was only to know what was most precious, he was to dwell in perfect happiness, he was not to become acquainted with pain and sorrow or with the misfortunes of life. He was protected from everything of that sort. It happened, however, that Josaphat one day went out of the palace and passed in succession a sick man, a leper, an aged man and a corpse—so runs the tale. He returned deeply moved into the king's palace and chanced upon a man whose soul was filled with the secrets of Christianity and whose name was Balaam; Balaam converted Josaphat, and this Josaphat who had experienced all this became a Christian.

It is not necessary to bring the Akashic Records to our aid in order to interpret this legend, since ordinary philology suffices to reveal the origin of the name Josaphat: Josaphat is derived from an old word Joaphat; Joaphat again from Joadosaph; Joadosaph from Juadosaph, which is identical with Budhasaph—both these last forms are Arabic—and Budhasaph is the same name as Bodhisattva. So the European occult teaching not only knows the Bodhisattva, it also knows, if it can decipher the name of Josaphat, the meaning of that word. This cultivation of occult knowledge in the West by means of legends contained the fact that there was a time when the being who lived in Gautama Buddha became a Christian. Whether this be a matter of knowledge or no, it is none the less true. Just as belated traditions may exist, as people may believe today that which was believed thousands of years ago and which has been propagated by means of tradition, so they may also believe that it accords with the laws of the higher worlds for Gautama Buddha to have remained the same as he was six hundred years before our era. But it is not so. He has ascended, he has evolved and in the true Rosicrucian teachings the knowledge of this fact has been preserved in the form of the above legend.

Within the spiritual life of Europe we find him who was the bearer of the Christ, Zarathas or Nazarathos—the original Zarathustra—appearing again from time to time. In the same way we meet with Skythianos again and the third great pupil of Manes, Buddha, as he was after he had taken part in the experiences of later ages.

Thus the European who had some knowledge of initiation looked into the changing ages and kept his gaze fixed on the true figures of the Great Teachers. He knew of Zarathas, of the Buddha, of Skythianos; he knew that through them wisdom was pouring into the civilization of the future—wisdom which had always proceeded from the Bodhisattvas and which must be used in order to promote understanding of the greatest treasure of all comprehension, the Christ, who is fundamentally a completely different Being from the Bodhisattvas and whom we can understand only by gathering together all the wisdom of the Bodhisattvas. Therefore in the spiritual wisdom of Europe there is a synthesis of all the teachings that have been given to the world through the three great pupils of Manes and by Manes himself. Even though people may not have understood Manes, a time will come when European civilization will take such form that there will be a feeling for what is connected with the names of Skythianos, the Buddha and Zarathustra. They give to mankind the material whose study will teach us to understand Christ, and through them our understanding of Him will grow more and more complete. The Middle Ages certainly showed a strange form of reverence and worship of Skythianos, the Buddha and Zarathustra when their names began to percolate through. In certain communities of the Christian religion anyone who wished to be taken for a true Christian had to utter the formula: 'I curse Skythianos, I curse the Buddha, I curse Zarathas!' But what it was then thought necessary to curse will become the centre for those who will best make Christ comprehensible to man, a central point to which mankind will look up as it did to the great Bodhisattvas through whom the Christ will be understood.

Today mankind can at the most bring two things to these teachings of the Rosy Cross—two things which may indicate a beginning of the power and greatness that will appear in the future in the form of the understanding of Christianity. Spiritual science of today will be the means of making one such beginning, by bringing the teachings of Skythianos, of Zarathustra, of Gautama Buddha to the world again, not in their old but in an absolutely new form, accessible to investigation from out of its very nature. The elements of what we learn from these three great Teachers must be embodied into civilization. From the Buddha, Christianity had to learn the teachings of reincarnation and of karma, but in the older religion they are to be found in an ancient guise unsuited to modern times. Why are the teachings of reincarnation and of karma flowing into Christianity today? Because the initiates have learned to understand them in a modern sense, just as the Buddha himself after his fashion understood them—and the Buddha was the great teacher of reincarnation. In the same way we shall attain to an understanding of Skythianos, whose teaching deals not only with the reincarnation of human beings but also with the powers which rule from eternity to eternity. So shall the central Being of the world, the Christ, be ever more and more understood. In this way the teachings of the initiates gradually flow into humanity.

The spiritual scientist of today can only bring two things in, as elementary beginnings compared to what must come about in the future spiritual evolution of mankind. The first element will be that which sinks into our innermost being in the form of the Christ life; and the second will be an increasingly comprehensive understanding of the Christ by the aid of spiritual cosmology. The Christ life in the inmost heart and an understanding of the world which leads to an understanding of Christ—these are the two elements. We may begin today, for we are only on the threshold of these things, by having the right feeling. We meet together for the purpose of cultivating right feeling about the spiritual world and all that is born out of it, as well as right feeling towards man. And as we cultivate this right feeling we gradually make our spiritual forces capable of receiving the Christ into our innermost being; for the higher and nobler our feelings become, the more nobly can Christ live within us. We make a beginning by teaching the elementary truths of our Earth evolution, by seeking that which we owe originally to Skythianos, Zarathustra and the Buddha, and by accepting it as they teach it in our age, in the form they themselves know it, their evolution having progressed to our present age. We have reached a point in civilization now where the elementary teachings of initiation are beginning to be disclosed.

A NOTE FROM RUDOLF STEINER PRESS

We are an independent publisher and registered charity (non-profit organisation) dedicated to making available the work of Rudolf Steiner in English translation. We care a great deal about the content of our books and have hundreds of titles available – as printed books, ebooks and in audio formats.

As a publisher devoted to anthroposophy...

- We continually commission translations of previously unpublished works by Rudolf Steiner and invest in re-translating, editing and improving our editions.

- We are committed to making anthroposophy available to all by publishing introductory books as well as contemporary research.

- Our new print editions and ebooks are carefully checked and proofread for accuracy, and converted into all formats for all platforms.

- Our translations are officially authorised by Rudolf Steiner's estate in Dornach, Switzerland, to whom we pay royalties on sales, thus assisting their critical work.

So, look out for Rudolf Steiner Press as a mark of quality and support us today by buying our books, or contact us should you wish to sponsor specific titles or to support the charity with a gift or legacy.

office@rudolfsteinerpress.com
Join our e-mailing list at www.rudolfsteinerpress.com

RUDOLF STEINER PRESS